HARCOURT SCIENCE

WORKBOOK

TEACHER'S EDITION

Harcourt School Publishers

Orlando • Boston • Dallas • Chicago • San Diego

www.harcourtschool.com

Harcourt

Contents

Harcourt

Harcourt

Safety in Science

Here are some safety rules to follow.

1 Think ahead. Study the steps and safety symbols of the investigation so you know what to expect. If you have any questions, ask your teacher.

2 Be neat. Keep your work area clean. If you have long hair, pull it back so it doesn't get in the way. Roll up long sleeves. If you should spill or break something, or get cut, tell your teacher right away.

3 Watch your eyes. Wear safety goggles when told to do so.

4 Yuck! Never eat or drink anything during a science activity unless you are told to do so by your teacher.

5 Don't get shocked. Be sure that electric cords are in a safe place where you can't trip over them. Don't ever pull a plug out of an outlet by pulling on the cord.

6 Keep it clean. Always clean up when you have finished. Put everything away and wash your hands.

Harcourt

In some activities you will see these symbols. They are signs for what you need to do to be safe.

CAUTION
Be especially careful.

CAUTION
Wear safety goggles.

CAUTION
Be careful with sharp objects.

CAUTION
Don't get burned.

CAUTION
Protect your clothes.

CAUTION
Protect your hands with mitts.

CAUTION
Be careful with electricity.

Science Safety

_____ I will study the steps of the investigation before I begin.

_____ I will ask my teacher if I do not understand something.

_____ I will keep my work area clean.

_____ I will pull my hair back and roll up long sleeves before I begin.

_____ I will tell my teacher if I spill or break something or get cut.

_____ I will wear safety goggles when I am told to do so.

_____ I will tell my teacher if I get something in my eye.

_____ I will not eat or drink anything during an investigation unless told to do so by my teacher.

_____ I will be extra careful when using electrical appliances.

_____ I will keep electric cords out of the way and only unplug them by pulling on the protected plug.

_____ I will clean up when I am finished.

_____ I will return unused materials to my teacher.

_____ I will wipe my area and then wash my hands.

Harcourt

Harcourt

Chapter 1 • Graphic Organizer for Chapter Concepts

How Plants Grow

LESSON 1
WHAT PLANTS ARE

plants need

1. air
2. water
3. soil
4. light

Plants are made of 5. _____ cells

LESSON 2
SIMPLE PLANTS

A simple plant has no

1. roots _____
2. stems _____
3. leaves _____

LESSON 2
PLANTS AND SEEDS

Needs of Seeds

1. warmth Warmth
2. water water

Plants Grow From

1. spores Pores
2. seeds seeds
3. other plant parts

Parts of a Seed

1. seed coat seed
2. seedling Seedling
3. food food

How Seeds Are Spread

1. air give
2. water water
3. animals animals

LESSON 3
FOOD FOR PLANTS

What Plants Need to Make Food

1. chlorophyll _____
2. sunlight _____
3. water _____
4. air, or carbon dioxide _____

How Plants Use Food

1. grow larger _____
2. store in stems, roots, and _____
   fruits _____

Name _____

Date _____

Needs of Plants

Materials

6 young plants   6 paper cups   potting soil   marker

brown paper bag   water   ruler

Activity Procedure

1 Put the plants in the paper cups and add soil. Make sure all six plants have the same amount of soil. Label two of the plants *No Water.* Put these plants in a sunny window.

2 Label two plants *No Light.* Place these plants on a table away from a window. Water the plants. Then cover them with a paper bag.

3 Label the last two plants *Water and Light.* Water these plants. Put them in a sunny window.

4 Every other day for two weeks, **observe** the plants. Check to make sure the plants labeled *No Light* and *Water and Light* have moist soil. Add enough water to keep the soil moist.

5 Record your observations on the chart on the next page. On the chart, **record** any changes you **observe** in the plants. Look for changes in the color and height of each plant.

Harcourt

Name _____

Plants	Day 1	Day 3	Day 5	Day 7	Day 9	Day 11
No Water						
No Light						
Water and Light						

Draw Conclusions

1. Which plants looked the healthiest after two weeks? the plants that got water and light _____

Why do you think so? The plants got what they needed to live and grow. _____

2. Which plants looked the least healthy after two weeks? Answers will vary; either the plants that did not get water or the ones that did not get light.

What was different for these plants? They did not receive everything they needed to live and grow. _____

3. Scientists at Work Scientists often **compare** observations to reach their conclusions. Compare your observations of the plants to tell what things plants need to grow. Make a list. Water, light, soil; some students may infer that plants need air, which they do. For students who do not realize that air is important to plants, lead them into a discussion that will elicit that idea.

Harcourt

Name _____

Date _____

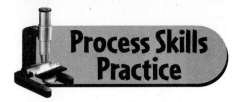

Process Skills Practice

Compare

When you compare, you identify how things are alike and how they are different. You can use your sense of sight when you compare. Comparing helps you gather information.

Think About Comparing

Suppose you plant two tomato plants in rich, dark soil in the back yard. You plant *Plant A* in a place where it gets full sun. You plant *Plant B* in a shady area. You give both plants the same amount of water. At the end of the growing season, *Plant A* is covered with juicy red tomatoes. *Plant B* has only a few tomatoes on it.

Plant A   **Plant B**

1. Compare the size of the two plants. Plant A is larger than Plant B.

_____

2. Compare the leaf color of the two plants. Students should infer that
Plant A will have leaves that are deep green. Plant B will have leaves
that are light green or yellowish.

3. How are the plants different from each other? Plant A is larger, has
more tomatoes, and has a healthier color than Plant B.

4. Which growing conditions were the same for both plants?
water and rich, dark soil

5. Which growing condition was different? amount of sunlight

_____

Harcourt

Use Context to Determine/Confirm Word Meaning

Read the paragraph below. Use your own words to write definitions for the underlined terms. Then use a dictionary to look up the terms. Compare your definitions with the dictionary definitions.

Healthful Foods

The leaves of many plants can be eaten as food. Many people enjoy eating lettuce, cabbage, or kale. Often, these leafy foods are eaten in salads along with other vegetables. Leafy vegetables are healthful and are good sources of fiber. Fiber cannot be digested, or broken down, but it helps food move through the intestines. Other plant foods that have fiber include Brussels sprouts, lentils, and avocados.

Your Own Words	Dictionary Definition
fiber _____ _____ _____	**fiber** an indigestible material in human food that stimulates the intestine
digested _____ _____ _____	**digested** the conversion of food into simpler chemical compounds that can be absorbed and used by
intestines _____ _____ _____ _____	**intestines** portion of the alimentary canal that extends from the stomach to the anus; in human beings and other mammals, it consists of two segments, the small intestine and the large intestine.

Harcourt

Name _____

Date _____

What Is a Plant?

Lesson Concept

Plants have a variety of needs that must be met in order
for them to live and grow.

Vocabulary

root (A7)	**stem** (A7)	**leaf** (A7)	**cell** (A8)

Underline the best answer.

1. Plants get what they need from the sun, air, rain, and ____.

   A plant food   **B** soil   **C** rocks   **D** animals

2. The stem of a plant supports the plant ____.

   A above ground   **C** underground

   B before it sprouts   **D** after it dies

3. Leaves help plants use ____.

   A light and air   **B** fruit   **C** soil   **D** food

**Write the name of the circled part of the plant under each
picture. Use the vocabulary list.**

4.

leaf
_____

5.

stem
_____

6.

roots
_____

Harcourt

The Parts of a Simple Plant

Materials

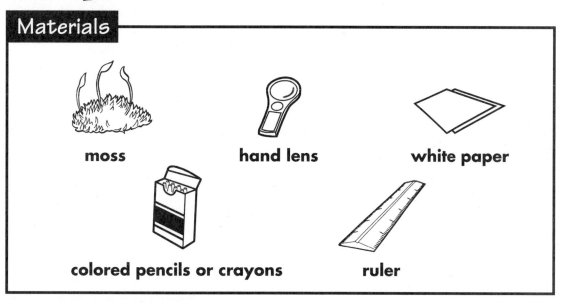

moss

hand lens

white paper

colored pencils or crayons

ruler

Activity Procedure

1 Feel a clump of moss. Describe how it feels. **Observe** it closely with a hand lens. Notice that it is made up of many tiny moss plants growing very close together. (Picture A)

2 Separate a single moss plant from the clump. Place it on a sheet of white paper. (Picture B)

3 **Observe** the stalk with the hand lens. Use colored pencils or crayons to make a drawing of the stalk. Label your drawing *stemlike part*.

4 **Observe** the tiny hairs growing from the bottom of the stemlike part. Add these to your drawing. Label them *rootlike parts*.

5 **Observe** the tiny green, leaflike parts growing around the stem. Feel their texture and thickness. Observe how they are arranged. Add these parts to your drawing. Label them *leaflike parts*.

6 Use the ruler to **measure** the height of the moss plant in millimeters. **Record** this height on your drawing.

Harcourt

Draw Conclusions

1. How is the moss plant like most plants you have seen?

A moss plant has parts that are similar to the roots, stems, and

leaves of common plants.

2. How is a moss plant different from most plants you have seen?

A moss's parts are much smaller than those of other plants; the soft,

leaflike structures are very thin and have no veins.

3. Scientists at Work Scientists use tools such as microscopes and hand lenses to **observe** living things more closely. What could you see with a hand lens that you could not see with your eyes alone?

Possible answers: Details in the rootlike, stemlike, and leaflike parts

were more visible with a hand lens; students may be able to see

more clearly—when using the hand lens—that the leaflike

structures do not have veins.

Investigate Further Peat moss comes from a type of moss that grows in swamps. Get a cup of dry peat moss and a cup of potting soil. **Record** the mass of each. **Form a hypothesis** about how much water each material can soak up. **Design and conduct an experiment** to test your hypothesis. **Infer** why peat moss is often added to garden soil.

_____

_____

_____

_____

_____

_____

Harcourt

Name _____

Date _____

Observe

When you observe, you use your senses. Sometimes you use all of your senses. At other times you may use only one or two of your senses. Using your senses can help you learn about something.

Think About Observing

Joanne takes a walk through a flower garden. She notices that there are many different types of flowers. They are different shapes, colors, and sizes. Some are big and bushy, while others grow tall. Some are small and grow low to the ground. Joanne observes many different colors. She smells some of the flowers. She feels a few of them. Some are fuzzy or smooth, others are prickly or rough. Joanne observes that each flower is different.

1. When you look at a flower garden, what can you observe?

Answers will vary. Plants have different shapes, sizes, and colors.

_____

2. What sense did you use in making this observation?

sight

_____

3. What other senses can you use to tell the different flowers apart?

touch, smell

_____

4. Blooming flowers sometimes attract bees. How can your sense of hearing help you make this observation?

Bees make a buzzing sound when they fly around the flower.

_____

5. Rose stems have thorns. What sense might this affect, and how?

touch; thorns are sharp and can cut or poke you.

_____

Use with page A13.

Harcourt

Identifying Supporting Facts and Details

Read the following paragraph. When you are finished, fill in the graphic organizer below, showing the main idea and supporting facts and details.

Where Simple Plants Grow Best

Because they have no roots, stems, or leaves, simple plants grow best in damp, shady places. Roots, stems and leaves have tubes that carry water to different parts of the plant. Simple plants do not have such tubes. They grow best where they can take their food, water, and nutrients directly from the environment. Without tubes to carry water long distances, they grow small and close to the ground.

Main Idea

Simple plants grow best in damp, shady places.

Supporting Fact

They do not have roots, stems, or leaves.

Supporting Fact

They do not have tubes to carry water and nutrients very far.

Supporting Fact

They take food directly from the environment.

Harcourt

What Parts Does a Simple Plant Have?

Lesson Concept

Simple plants have a different form than other plants, such as trees and flowers, do.

Vocabulary

simple plants (A14)	**leaves** (A14)	**roots** (A14)
environment (A14)	**mosses** (A14)	**tubes** (A14)
liverworts (A14)	**stems** (A14)	

Fill in the blanks below, using vocabulary terms from above.

_____ do not grow very big. Simple plants have

no _____, _____, or

_____. Unlike trees and flowers, simple plants do not

have _____ to move water and nutrients to every part.

A simple plant takes in nutrients from its _____.

_____ and _____ are

simple plants.

Harcourt

Name _____

Date _____

Sprouting Seeds

Materials

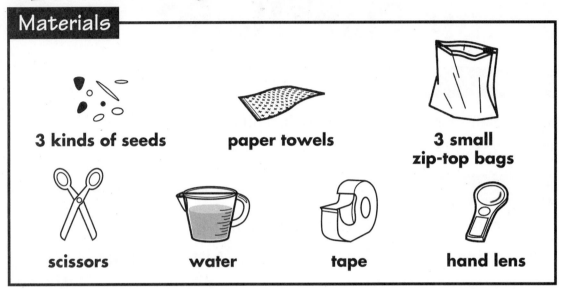

3 kinds of seeds   paper towels   3 small zip-top bags

scissors   water   tape   hand lens

Activity Procedure

1 Start with a small amount of mixed seeds. Use size and shape to sort the seeds into three groups.

2 Cut two paper towels in half. Fold the towels to fit into the plastic bags. Add water to make the towels damp. Do not use too much water or you will drown the seeds.

3 Put one group of seeds into each bag, and seal the bags. Label the bags *1*, *2*, and *3*. Tape the bags to the inside of a window.

4 Use a hand lens to **observe** the seeds every school day for 10 days. Use the chart below and on the next page to **record** your observations.

Seeds	Days				
	1	2	3	4	5
Group 1					
Group 2					
Group 3					

Harcourt

Name _____

Seeds	Days				
	6	7	8	9	10
Group 1					
Group 2					
Group 3					

Draw Conclusions

1. What changes did you **observe** in the seeds? Roots and other plant parts grew from the seeds.

2. How quickly did the changes take place in the different kinds of seeds?
Answers will vary, but the first changes should occur on about Day 2.

3. Scientists at Work Scientists **observe** their investigations closely to get new information. How did observing the seeds help you understand more about seeds? It helped me understand how seeds grow.

Investigate Further Repeat the investigation steps, but place the bags in a dark closet instead of in a window. **Predict** what will happen. **Record** your observations.

My prediction: Students will probably predict that the seeds will not germinate in a dark closet because they will not get the light they need. Remind them that most seeds germinate underground, where there is no light.

My observations: Students should find that seeds germinate in a dark closet but that the plants that grow are white, or very light green. This is because chlorophyll, the green coloring matter in plants, needs sunlight to develop.

Harcourt

Name _____

Date _____

Observe

You can observe directly with
your senses. Or you can use a
hand lens or microscope to
observe. Making an observation
is one of the most basic science skills.

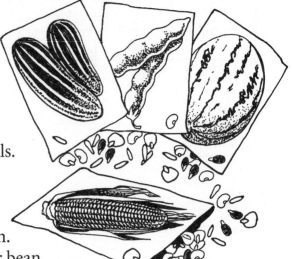

Think About Observing

You are planning a vegetable garden.
You order watermelon, corn, butter bean,
and cucumber seeds. When the seeds arrive,
they are all mixed together in one container! The company has sent colored
pictures of the seeds and the vegetables that will grow from the seeds. You
can use your observation skills to identify the seeds.

1. You spread the seeds out on a table. Which sense will you use to observe
the seeds? ___sight_____

2. In what ways are the seeds different from one another?
Answers will vary. Students should list size, pattern, and shape;
some may suggest that the seeds are different colors.

3. How could a hand lens help you with your observations?
It could help you observe the seeds more closely.

4. Describe what you will do to match the seeds to the seeds in the picture.

Step 1: Possible sequence: Look closely at the pictures of the seeds.

Step 2: Look closely at the seeds in the pile.

Step 3: Sort the seeds based on observed differences.

5. How did observing help you understand which seeds were which?
Observing the seeds provided information that allowed me to sort
the seeds into groups.

Harcourt

Use with page A17.

Name _____

Date _____

Use Graphic Sources for Information

Seeds

Label the parts of the seed. Use the descriptions below.

Seedling: A seedling lives inside every seed.

Seed coat: The seed coat protects the young plant inside the seed.

Stored food: Most of the inside of a seed is stored food. The young plant uses the food to grow when the seed sprouts.

These plants form seeds. Color in and label where each seed should be.

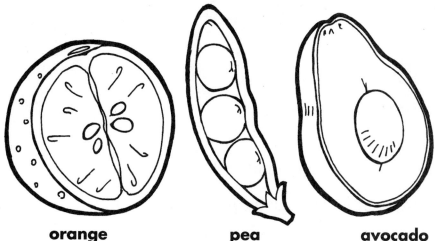

orange   **pea**   **avocado**

Seeds of orange should be colored; inside the pod, the peas should be colored; the large seed in the avocado should be colored.

Harcourt

Name _____

Date _____

What Kinds of Plants Have Seeds?

Lesson Concept

Seeds produce seedlings that grow into new plants.

Vocabulary

seeds (A18)   **germinate** (A21)   **seedlings** (A21)

Fill in the blank with the correct vocabulary term from the list above.

Some plants form _____ *seeds* _____ to make new plants.

The small new plants are called _____ *seedlings* _____. Some plants also can be grown from plant parts. Seeds grow to look like the adult plants they came from. All seeds have the same parts. Seeds need water to _____ *germinate* _____. Seeds are spread to new places by air, water, and animals.

For each picture below circle the plant part that makes seeds.

These sentences are mixed up. Number them in order.

__2__ The sprout breaks through the soil.

__3__ Leaves begin to grow.

__1__ A root grows from the seed.

Use with page A25.

Harcourt

Name _____

Date _____

Food Factories

Harcourt

Materials

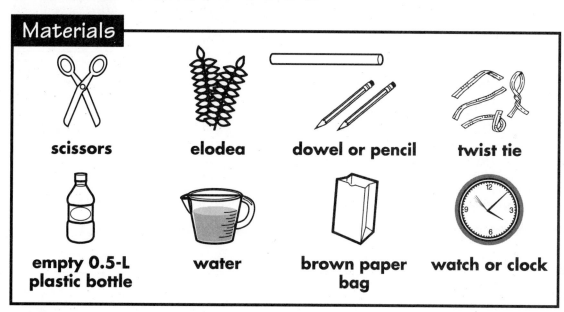

scissors	elodea	dowel or pencil	twist tie
empty 0.5-L plastic bottle	water	brown paper bag	watch or clock

Activity Procedure

1 **CAUTION** **Be careful when using scissors.** Use scissors to cut a piece of elodea (el•oh•DEE•uh) as long as the bottle.

2 Wrap the elodea around the dowel. Use a twist tie to attach it to the dowel.

3 Put the elodea into the bottle, and fill the bottle with water.

4 Put the bottle in a place away from any windows. Cover the bottle with the brown paper bag. After 10 minutes, remove the bag. **Record** any changes you **observe.**

My observations: _____

_____

5 This time, place the bottle in bright sunlight and don't cover it with the brown paper bag. After 10 minutes, **observe** the bottle. **Record** any changes you observe.

My observations: _____

_____

Draw Conclusions

1. Did the elodea and water in the bottle look different after Steps 4 and 5?

yes _____ If they did, tell how they were different.

At the end of Step 5, there were bubbles in the water.

2. What did you change between Steps 4 and 5? What remained the same in steps 4 and 5?

The plant was moved from darkness into light. The plant was still

in water.

3. Scientists at Work From what you **observed**, what can you **infer** about

the bubbles you saw? The bubbles came from the plant when it was in

the light but not when it was in the dark. So the bubbles must

have something to do with light.

Investigate Further Scientists often **measure** what happens in experiments. One way to measure what is happening in this experiment is to count the number of bubbles that appear. Put the bottle with the elodea in bright sunlight, and count the number of bubbles that appear in one minute.

My observations: Students should observe many bubbles when the

plant is in direct sunlight.

Then move the bottle out of the direct sun. Again count the number of bubbles that appear in one minute.

My observations: Students should observe fewer bubbles when the

plant is not in direct sunlight.

How are the two measurements different? **Infer** why they are different.

There were more bubbles when the plant was in sunlight. Sunlight

made a difference in the amount of gas the plant produced.

Harcourt

Name _____

Date _____

Infer

When you infer, you use what you have observed to form an opinion or give an explanation. That opinion is called an inference.

Think About Inferring

You and your friend are having a contest to see who can grow the tallest sunflower. You each plant a seed in your backyard. The seeds germinate and begin to grow. You both give your plants water and fertilizer. The two flowers grow taller every day. One day you go out to check your sunflower. You observe that the petals of your sunflower have holes in them. You use your hand lens to examine the whole plant from the flower to where the stem goes into the ground. You see a worm crawling on the flower.

1. What are you trying to explain? _what is making holes in the flower petals_

2. What are your observations? _Observations should include holes in the flower petals and a worm crawling on the flower._

3. What information did you gather? _A worm was on the flower._

4. What could you infer about the holes in the petal of the sunflower? How would you explain them? _Students will likely infer that the holes were caused by the worm eating the flowers._

5. Think about your inference. Do you think your plant will grow or die? Explain your opinion. _Accept reasonable answers. Some students may suggest that if damage continues, the flower may die. Others may say that the damage isn't large enough to cause the plant to die._

Harcourt

Name _____

Date _____

Arrange Events in Sequence

Look at the sentences below. Reorder the sentences and write a paragraph using the sentences.

The plant uses some of the food to grow bigger and make seeds.

People and animals use some of these plant parts as food.

The plant makes sugar and gives off oxygen.

Some plants store some of this food in their roots, stems, and fruits.

A plant takes in sunlight, water, and carbon dioxide.

The chlorophyll in the leaves lets the plant use these things to make food.

A plant takes in sunlight, water, and carbon dioxide. The chlorophyll in the leaves lets the plant use these things to make food. The plant makes sugar and gives off oxygen. The plant uses some of the food to grow bigger and make seeds. Some plants store some of this food in their roots, stems, and fruits. People and animals use some of these plant parts as food.

_____

Harcourt

Use with page A30.

Name _____

Date _____

How Do Plants Make Food?

Lesson Concept

Plants make their own food through the process of photosynthesis.

Vocabulary

photosynthesis (A28)	**chlorophyll** (A28)

For each pair of sentences, circle the letter of the correct statement.

1. A The substance in plants that makes them green is called photosynthesis.

　　B The substance in plants that makes them green is called chlorophyll.

2. A Photosynthesis is the process plants use to make carbon dioxide.

　　B Photosynthesis is the process plants use to make food.

3. A Plants use the food they make to grow bigger and make seeds.

　　B Plants use the food they make to produce carbon dioxide.

Circle the parts of each plant where food that humans eat is stored.

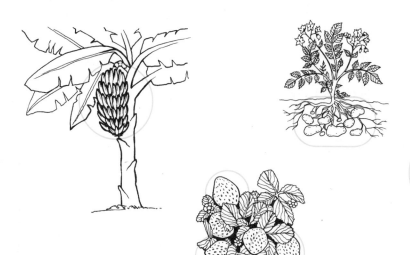

Use with page A31.

Name _____

Date _____

Recognize Vocabulary

root	cell	seed	leaves	stem
germinate	chlorophyll	photosynthesis	seedling	

Use the words above to fill in the blanks in the paragraph.

   Two classmates decided to grow two plants for the science fair. First, they filled two clear plastic pots with good soil. They planted one _____ seed _____ in each pot. They placed one pot in a sunny window and the other in a closet. They observed their plants each day.

   The seeds began to _____ germinate _____. One day the classmates saw a _____ root _____ growing down into the dirt of each pot. Next, a young plant called a _____ seedling _____ appeared. Each plant was supported by a _____ stem _____.

   The classmates observed that the plant in the closet was no longer doing well. Its _____ leaves _____ were not green. The _____ chlorophyll _____ in the plant needed sun to help the plant make food. The process of _____ photosynthesis _____ could not continue in the _____ cell _____ without light.

Draw the stages of the growth of plants. Label each picture. On the last picture, label as many plant parts as you can.

Students should draw a seed.	Students should draw a sprouting seed.	Students should draw an adult plant and label root (if visible), stem, leaf, and flowers.
_____	_____	_____

Harcourt

Use with pages A4–A31.

Writing Practice

Compare and Contrast Plants

Informative Writing–Compare and Contrast

Observe two different plants that grow from seeds. Then write a
paragraph comparing and contrasting the two plants. Use the
chart below to help you list ways the two plants are alike and ways
they are different.

Plant 1	Plant 1 and Plant 2	Plant 2
Different	Alike	Different
Big Big 2BW		

Harcourt

Chapter 2 • Graphic Organizer for Chapter Concepts

Types of Animals

LESSON 1

Animal Needs
1. food
2. water
3. shelter
4. air

LESSON 2

	covered with	breathe with	how born
Mammals	1. fur	2. lungs	3. live birth
Birds	4. feathers	5. lungs	6. hatch from eggs

LESSON 3

	covered with	breathe with	how born
Amphibians	1. smooth, moist skin	2. gills, then lungs	3. hatch from eggs
Fish	4. scales	5. gills	6. most hatch
Reptiles	7. dry skin and scales	8. lungs	9. most hatch

LESSON 4

Animal Behaviors Are
1. learned
2. instinct

To Escape the Cold, Animals
3. migrate
4. hibernate

Animals Are Protected By
5. camouflage
6. mimicry

LESSON 5

Extinction: Species can be
1. threatened
2. endangered
3. extinct

Harcourt

Name _____

Date _____

Animal Homes

Materials

Animal Picture Cards

Activity Procedure

1 Select six Animal Picture Cards, or use the pictures on page A40. As you **observe** the cards, pay close attention to the types of homes the animals live in.

2 Describe each animal home you **observe. Record** your descriptions.

Animal Home 1: _Descriptions will vary depending on animal homes selected._____

Animal Home 2: _____

Animal Home 3: _____

Animal Home 4: _____

Animal Home 5: _____

Animal Home 6: _____

3 With a partner, discuss the different types of animal homes shown. Talk about the ways the animal homes are alike and the ways they are different. Then **classify** the animals by the types of homes they live in.

Harcourt

Name _____

Investigate Log

My Classification	
Description	**Animals in the Group**

Draw Conclusions

1. Compare two of the animal homes you observed. Tell how each home helps protect the animal that lives there. Answers will vary, depending on the animal homes selected. _____

_____

2. What did you **observe** about the home of a Canada goose and the home of an albatross? Both the Canada goose and the albatross build nests as their homes. _____

_____

3. Scientists at Work Scientists **classify** animals into groups based on what the animals have in common. How many groups did you classify the animals into? What were the groups? Answers may vary, but will likely indicate three groups. The groups may be animals that live in nests, animals that have shells or other structures that provide shelter, and animals that use holes as shelters. Accept all logical responses.

Investigate Further Study the Animal Picture Cards again. This time, look at the body covering of each animal. Describe each covering. How can you use body coverings to **classify** animals? Answers will vary but may include grouping animals as those with fur, those with feathers, and those that have shells or shell-like coverings.

Harcourt

Name _____

Date _____

Classify

Classifying is putting objects into groups according to how they are alike.

Think About Classifying

Your teacher gives you a worksheet showing different animals. You must classify the animals. You decide to classify them based on how they move. In the chart below, list the animals based on how they move.

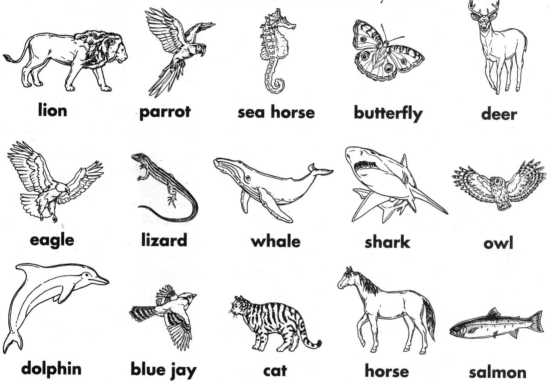

Classifying Animals by How They Move		
Walking Animals	**Flying Animals**	**Swimming Animals**
lion	eagle	whale
cat	blue jay	dolphin
deer	parrot	sea horse
lizard	owl	salmon
horse	butterfly	shark

Use with page A41.

Name _____

Date _____

Compare and Contrast

Animals need air, water, food, and shelter. Different animals meet their needs in different ways. Use the information below to answer the questions.

Brown Bear • eats plants such as grasses or berries • catches and eats fish	**Robin** • builds nest of leaves, moss, and feathers • uses lungs to breathe
Panda • lives in a mountain forest • eats bamboo plants	**Turtle** • uses its hard shell as its home • eats insects, worms, berries, and mushrooms
Beaver • builds its dam in a stream • uses cut trees, rocks, and mud for dam • uses lungs to breathe	**Whale** • lives in water • uses lungs to breathe

1. Which three animals named above eat plants?

brown bear, panda, turtle

2. How is the home of a turtle different from the home of a robin?

A turtle uses its shell. A robin finds other materials and builds a nest.

3. How might a robin and a beaver be similar in the way they build their homes?

Both a robin and a beaver find materials to build their homes.

4. Do pandas and brown bears eat the same kinds of food? Explain.

No. Pandas eat bamboo plants. Brown bears eat grasses, berries, and fish.

5. How are a whale and a bird similar?

Both a whale and a bird breathe with lungs.

Harcourt

Name _____

Date _____

What Is an Animal?

Lesson Concept

All animals have needs that must be met in order for them to live.

Vocabulary

traits (A48)   **inherit** (A48)

Fill in each blank with a vocabulary term.

All animals need food, water, air, and shelter. Different animals have different shapes and sizes. They have many different body parts. These shapes, sizes, and different body parts help animals get the things they need.

All animals _____ their features from their parents.

These features are called _____ .

Underline the best answer.

1. The four things that all animals need are ____.
   A food, water, shelter, and air   **C** food, water, heat, and air
   B food, water, sunlight, and air   **D** soil, water, food, and sunlight

2. Animals that live on land get oxygen from ____.
   A the air   **B** food   **C** water   **D** sunlight

3. An animal's body produces energy from ____.
   A coal   **B** food   **C** air   **D** sunlight

4. The bodies of all animals contain ____.
   A water   **B** feathers   **C** fur   **D** scales

5. Caves, nests, turtle shells, and tunnels are all examples of ____.
   A animal shelters   **C** inherited traits
   B food containers   **D** water sources

Harcourt

Name _____

Date _____

Fur Helps Animals

Materials

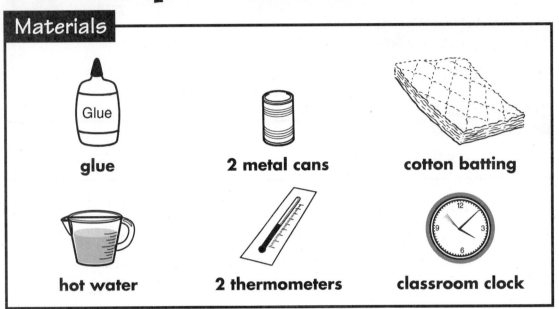

glue

2 metal cans

cotton batting

hot water

2 thermometers

classroom clock

 CAUTION **Activity Procedure**

1 Record your observations on the chart on the next page.

2 Spread glue around the outside of one can. Then put a thick layer of cotton around the can. Wait for the glue to dry. Then use your fingers to fluff the cotton.

3 **CAUTION** **Be careful with the hot water, it can burn you.** Your teacher will fill both cans with hot water.

4 Place a thermometer in each can, and **record** the temperature of the water.

5 Check the temperature of the water in each can every 10 minutes for a period of 30 minutes. **Record** the temperatures on the chart.

Harcourt

Time	Water Temperature in Can with Cotton	Water Temperature in Can Without Cotton
Start		
10 min		
20 min		
30 min		

Draw Conclusions

1. In which can did the water stay hot longer? Why? The can with cotton. The cotton helped keep the water warm.

2. How is having fur like wearing a jacket? Fur helps keep animals warm the same way clothes or a jacket helps a human stay warm.

3. Scientists at Work Scientists often **use a model** to study things they can't observe easily. In this investigation, you made a model of an animal with fur. Why was using a model easier than observing an animal? It would be impossible to test an animal with and without fur to find out what the fur does.

Investigate Further How do you think your results would be different if you used ice-cold water instead of hot water? Write a **hypothesis** and **conduct an experiment** to find out.

My hypothesis: Predictions and hypotheses will vary but will likely state that the water in the cotton-covered can will maintain its temperature longer.

Name _____

Date _____

Use a Model

Using a model can help you study things you cannot observe easily.

Think About Using a Model

A polar bear has black skin. The polar bear's skin takes in the heat from the sun. You decide to make a model to test this idea. On a warm, sunny day, you take four ice cubes out of the freezer. You wrap two ice cubes in black plastic and two in white plastic. You put the two packets on a tray and set it outside in the sun. You want to find out which packet of ice cubes absorbs the heat more quickly. You time which packet of ice cubes melts faster. You feel each packet at five-minute intervals. You find out that the ice in the black plastic melted faster than the ice in the white plastic.

1. Why would you use a model to find out about the heat absorption of the polar bear's skin? because you can't use the actual skin without harming a polar bear

2. What observations can you make? You can see water collecting as the ice melts; you can feel how the temperatures of the two packets change as they sit in the sun.

3. What comparisons can you make between the two packets? the amount of water that collects; the amount of time it takes for each ice cube to melt; the relative warmth of each packet

4. Use your observations to infer why the ice in the black packet melted faster than the ice in the white packet. The only difference between the two packets is the color plastic they were wrapped in. So the black color must have warmed faster, causing the ice to melt faster.

5. What might this model tell you about the polar bear's skin? Black skin will likely warm faster than white skin would. This will help keep the polar bear warm in its cold climate.

Harcourt

Use with page A51.

Name _____

Date _____

Summarize and Paraphrase a Selection

Bird Beaks and Feet

You can learn a lot about a bird by looking at its beak and its feet. The shape of a bird's beak can tell you what that bird eats. For example, a pelican is a water bird with a pouch that extends from its throat. The pelican uses its beak and throat pouch to scoop up fish, much like we use a net to catch fish. Many vultures have strong, heavy beaks, which they use for tearing at meat, such as the carcass of a dead animal.

The shape of a bird's feet can tell you where a bird lives. A loon has webbed feet that allow it to dive and swim long distances underwater. A penguin doesn't fly, so it must rely on its feet for movement. The feet of a penguin are located close to its tail, allowing the penguin to walk upright on the ice where it lives.

1. What would be two headings you would use to describe the above section?

Beaks; Feet

2. Write a brief summary of the above selection.

Beaks and feet can tell you a lot about a bird. The shape of a bird's beak can tell you what that bird eats. The shape of a bird's feet can be used to tell where it lives.

Use with pages A46.

What Are Mammals and Birds?

Lesson Concept

Most mammals have fur or hair, and give birth to live young. Most birds have feathers and lay eggs from which young are hatched.

Vocabulary

mammals (A52)   **birds** (A55)

Match each phrase with the best answer. Write the letter of the best answer on the line. Some may have more than one answer.

B, C, D, F, G **1.** These are traits mammals share.

E, G **2.** Birds are grouped based on the shape of these features.

A **3.** These cover most of a bird's body.

A feathers
B fur or hair
C lungs to breathe
D usually give birth to live young
E beaks
F feed their young with milk made in their bodies
G feet

Label each mammal with an *M*. Label each bird with a *B*.

4. __M__   **5.** __B__   **6.** __M__

7. __B__   **8.** __B__   **9.** __M__

Harcourt

From Egg to Frog

Materials

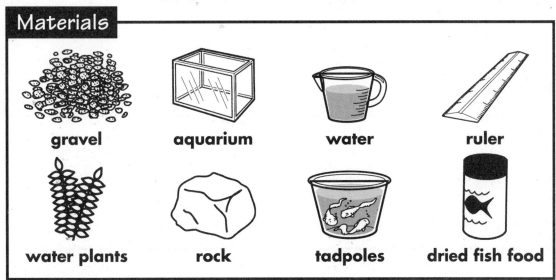

gravel   aquarium   water   ruler

water plants   rock   tadpoles   dried fish food

Activity Procedure

1 Put a layer of gravel on the bottom of the aquarium. Add 12 cm to 15 cm of water.

2 Float some water plants on top of the water, and stick others into the gravel. Add the rock. It should be big enough so that frogs can sit on it later and be out of the water.

3 Put two or three tadpoles, or young frogs, in the water. Put the aquarium where there is some light but no direct sunlight.

4 Feed the tadpoles a small amount of dried fish food once a day. Add fresh water to the aquarium once a week.

5 **Observe** the tadpoles every day. Once a week, make a drawing of what they look like. Use the charts below and on the next page for your data.

	Observations	Drawing
Day 1		
Day 2		
Day 3		
Day 4		
Day 5		

Harcourt

Name _____

	Observations	Drawing
Day 6		
Day 7		
Day 8		
Day 9		
Day 10		
Day 11		
Day 12		
Day 13		
Day 14		
Day 15		

Draw Conclusions

1. What changes did you see as the tadpoles grew? The tadpoles grew back legs and then front legs. As the tadpoles developed into frogs, their tails began to shrink.

2. When the tadpoles began to climb out of the water, what did their bodies look like? The tadpoles came out of the water once they had grown four legs. They stayed out longer and longer as their tails shrank.

3. Scientists at Work Scientists **record** what they **observe**. How did recording your observations help you learn about the growing tadpoles?
Recording helped me remember how the tadpoles changed.

Investigate Further How important were the water plants to the growth of the tadpoles? **Form a hypothesis** about this question, and **plan an experiment** to test your hypothesis.
Students' hypotheses will vary. Suggested experiments will likely use similar equipment and follow the same procedures as outlined in this activity but will eliminate the addition of plants to the aquarium.

Harcourt

Name _____

Date _____

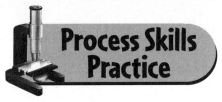

Observe and Record

When you **observe** something, you use your senses of sight, hearing, smell, and touch. You can **record** your observations.

Think About Observing and Recording

Eva has a fish tank with tropical fish living in it. One day she notices that the glass sides of the tank have green matter on them. The filter is much too loud. An unpleasant smell is coming from the water. The side of the tank feels cold. She doesn't hear the hum of the heater that keeps the water warm.

1. Count how many times she used each of her senses in observing her fish tank. Record the numbers in the columns.

Sight	Hearing	Smell	Touch	Taste
/	//		/	

2. **Record** what Eva saw.

   She saw: green matter on the tank sides.

3. **Record** what Eva heard (or did not hear).

   She heard: the loud water filter.

   She missed hearing: the hum of the heater.

4. **Record** what Eva smelled, touched, and tasted.

   Smell: water smelled bad

   Touch: tank felt cold

   Taste: did not use sense of taste at all; tasted nothing

5. Use all these observations to suggest what is wrong with the tank.

   The heater quit working. Some type of green living thing grew. Fish

   waste built up in the poorly filtered water, making the water smell.

Harcourt

Name _____

Date _____

Arrange Events in Sequence

Sea Horses and Their Young

The following sentences describe how a sea horse reproduces. The sentences are out of sequence. Match the sentence with the number to show what you think the sequence should be. Then use some of the signal words in the box to rewrite the sentences in paragraph form.

1. The female sea horse deposits fertilized eggs into a special pouch of the male sea horse. The pouch is located near the tail of the sea horse. The eggs remain in the pouch until they are hatched. 1

2. The eggs hatch. 2

3. The young sea horses are pushed out through an opening in the pouch. 4

4. The sea horse is distinctive because the male, not the female, carries the eggs. 3

Signal Words:	first	next	finally

The sea horse is distinctive because the male, not the female, carries the eggs. First, the female sea horse deposits fertilized eggs into a special pouch of the male sea horse. The pouch is located near the tail of the sea horse. The eggs remain in the pouch until they are hatched. Next, the eggs hatch. Finally, the young sea horses are pushed out through an opening in the pouch.

Harcourt

Name _____

Date _____

 **Concept Review**

What Are Amphibians, Fish, and Reptiles?

Lesson Concept

Amphibians begin life in water, fish live all their lives in water, and reptiles are land animals.

Vocabulary

amphibians (A60) **gills** (A61) **fish** (A62)

scales (A62) **reptiles** (A63)

Fill in each blank with a vocabulary term.

Animals that begin life in water, change in form, and then live on land are

called _____. _____ live in the

water, use _____ for breathing, and have body parts

that help them swim. _____ are land animals that are

covered with _____.

Label each animal as *amphibian, fish,* or *reptile*. Circle the animals that have gills at some time during their lives. Cross out the animals that always breathe with lungs.

 **lizard**   **tadpole**  **salmon**

1. _____ 2. _____ 3. _____

 **turtle**  **shark**  **toad**

4. _____ 5. _____ 6. _____

Harcourt

Use with page A65.

How Animals Hide

Materials

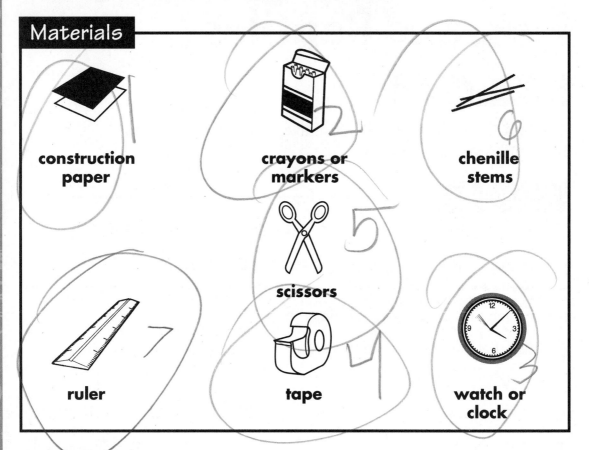

construction paper

crayons or markers

chenille stems

scissors

ruler

tape

watch or clock

Activity Procedure

1. Choose a place in the room to put your insect. Note the color and shape of objects in that place. Decide what color and shape your insect should be to blend in.

2. Your insect should be at least 5 cm long and 3 cm wide. Use a ruler to draw a rectangle this size. Draw the shape of your insects inside the rectangle. (Picture A)

3. Color your insect. Use colors and patterns that blend in with the place you chose for your insect.

4. Place your insect. It should be in full view and not hidden behind anything. If necessary, use tape to hold it in place. (Picture B)

5. When all the insects are placed, ask someone from another class to be a bird. Tell the "bird" to find as many insects as he or she can in one minute. Record in the chart the number found.

Harcourt

6. Give the bird another minute to find more insects. Record the number found. Continue until all the insects have been found.

Minute	Number of Insects Found
1	1
2	2
3	3

Draw Conclusions

1. Which insects were found first? How could they have been hidden better?

Possible answer: The insects that were found quickly had contrasting colors, patterns, or shapes that stood out against the background.

2. Which insects were found last? Why were they so hard to see?

Possible response: The insects that were not found quickly had colors, patterns, or shapes that blended in well with their surroundings.

3. **Scientists at Work** Scientists **observe** animals closely to see how they blend in with their environment. How did observing help you understand how insects' shapes and colors help them do this?

Students should have discovered different ways that insects can blend in with their environment. For example, some insects may be similar in color to their backgrounds, some may have patterns that help them blend in with their environment, and some may have shapes similar to items in their environment.

Harcourt

Name _____

Date _____

Make a Model

Scientists often make a model of a process or an object in nature. This helps them to closely **observe** processes or objects that usually could not be studied easily in nature.

Think About Making a Model

Animals often take on the color, shape, or pattern of their environment. Cut two pieces of paper 4 cm square. Color one with black stripes. Color the other with black dots of assorted sizes.

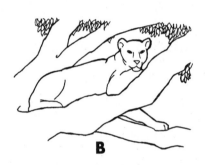

1. Place the rectangle that you have colored with a black-stripe pattern over the animal in Picture A and then over the animal in Picture B. Which animal does this pattern help hide? Why does this pattern work well with this environment?

The stripe pattern would help the animal in Picture A hide better

because it would be hard to see the stripes of the animals against

the stripes of the long grass.

2. Place the rectangle that you have colored with a black-dot pattern over the animal in Picture A and then over the animal in Picture B. Which animal does this pattern help hide? Why does this pattern work well with this environment?

The dot pattern would help the animal in Picture B hide because

it would be hard to see the dots on the animal against the spots

of shade.

Use with page A67.

Name _____

Date _____

Identify Cause and Effect

Bats in Winter

   In some regions, insect-eating bats have trouble finding food in winter. Some make long-distance trips to warmer places. Others spend the winter hibernating in caves. The bat's body temperature drops during hibernation, which means that the animal needs less food. During the winter, when there are no insects available, the bat will live off its body fat.

Read the selection above, and then identify the causes and effects.

Cause		Effect
winter	→	hibernate in caves
body temperature drops	→	needs less food
insects not available	→	lives off body fat

Harcourt

Concept Review

How Do Animals Behave?

Lesson Concept

Most animals have behavior that is both instinctive and learned. Some of these instincts help animals avoid danger. Write the word under each picture that describes the behavior of the animal.

Vocabulary

instinct (A68)
hibernate (A69)

migrate (A70)
camouflage (A72)
mimicry (A72)

instinct
_____

hibernate
_____

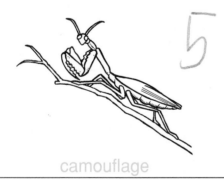

camouflage
_____

mimicry
_____

migrate
_____

Use with page A73.

Harcourt

Endangered Animals

Materials

reference books   **graph paper**   **ruler**

Activity Procedure

1. Find a list of endangered species from reference books or the Internet.

2. Choose five endangered animals from the lists. Look for information about how the numbers of these animals have changed over time. Find out how many of each animal are living now.

3. Make a bar graph for your animals. For each animal, draw one bar to show how many were alive 10 years ago. Use a second bar to show how many are alive now.

4. Infer what will happen in the future to the animals on your graph. Explain your inferences, and share them with the class.

Harcourt

Investigate Log

Draw Conclusions

1. How did **using numbers** help you **organize your data** in this activity?

Possible answers: Rather than just saying that populations

increased or decreased, I was able to make a graph to show

how much the populations changed over time.

2. What could happen that would change your **prediction**? **Record** your ideas. New data might indicate that a population is moving in the

opposite direction of the first one reported.

3. Scientists at Work Scientists **use numbers** to help them **organize their data**. They then use their data to make inferences. How did making a bar graph help you make your prediction about the future of the animals?

Looking at the bar graph, I could see what direction the population

was moving in (up or down) and infer where I thought the

population was going.

Investigate Further Animals are not the only kinds of organisms that can become endangered. Find information on five kinds of plants that are endangered, and make a bar graph as you did for the animals.

Species may include Santa Cruz cypress, Presidio manzanita,

Bakersfield cactus, or Catalina island mountain-mahogany.

Harcourt

Name _____

Date _____

Use Numbers and Infer

When you use numbers, you can summarize and try to understand data in a table. When you infer, you form an opinion about what the numbers show. The opinion is called an inference.

Think About Inferring and Using Numbers

The table below shows the populations of wolves and deer in an area between 1900 and 1940. The wolf and deer populations stayed about the same before 1900. Then sheep farmers began killing the wolves. Without predators, the deer population started to increase. Review the information in the table. Then use it to answer the questions below.

	Wolf Population	Deer Population
1900	850	10,000
1910	500	15,000
1920	400	22,000
1930	100	27,000
1940	10	36,000

1. Use numbers to explain what happened to the deer population.
It increased by 26,000.

2. Use numbers to explain what happened to the wolf population.
It decreased by 840.

3. What can you infer about why deer increased in population while wolves decreased? Students can infer that wolves eat deer. As the number of wolves decreased, fewer deer were eaten. The deer population were

then increased.

Harcourt

Name _____

Date _____

Reading Skills Practice

Use Reference Sources

Use an encyclopedia or on-line resource to determine whether each of the following animals is threatened, endangered, or extinct.

Animal	Status
California Condor	endangered
Snow Leopard	endangered
Dodo	extinct
Bald Eagle	threatened
Passenger Pigeon	extinct
Japanese Giant Salamander	endangered

Choose an endangered species to research. Find out the causes of the animals endangerment and what is being done to protect this animal. Report your findings to the class.

_____

_____

_____

_____

_____

_____

Harcourt

Concept Review

What Is Extinction?

Lesson Concept

Sometimes animal species become extinct. Extinction can be natural. People can also cause extinction. Laws protect some animals that are in danger of becoming extinct.

Vocabulary

extinct (A76)   **endangered** (A76)   **fossil** (A77)

species (A76)   **threatened** (A77)

Underline the best answer.

1. Evidence of an animal or plant that lived long ago is a(n) ____.
   A fossil   **B** species   **C** organism   **D** rock

2. A ____ is a type of organism.
   A species   **B** habitat   **C** population   **D** fossil

3. A species that no longer exists is ____.
   A endangered   **B** threatened   **C** extinct   **D** growing

4. Most species become extinct today because their ____ is destroyed.
   A predator   **B** habitat   **C** food   **D** mate

5. A species that is in danger of becoming extinct is ____.
   A threatened   **B** endangered   **C** healthy   **D** stable

6. There are ____ to protect threatened and endangered animals.
   A predators   **B** species   **C** hunters   **D** laws

7. A species that is on its way to becoming endangered or extinct is ____.
   A threatened   **B** dead   **C** increasing   **D** fossilized

Name _____

Date _____

Recognize Vocabulary

Match the definitions on the left with the terms on the right.

__C__   **1.** animal that lives in water its whole life

__D__   **2.** body parts that take in oxygen from the water

__F__   **3.** animal that has fur or hair

__E__   **4.** how animals get traits from their parents

__B__   **5.** animal that has feathers, wings, and two legs

__G__   **6.** land animal with dry skin, covered with scales

__A__   **7.** animal that begins life in water and moves on to land as an adult

__I__   **8.** a body feature an animal inherits

__H__   **9.** small, thin, flat plates that help protect fish

__L__   **10.** steadily going down in number

__M__   **11.** evidence of an organism that lived long ago

__K__   **12.** gone forever

__N__   **13.** in danger of becoming extinct

__J__   **14.** group of related organisms

A amphibian
B bird
C fish
D gills
E inherit
F mammal
G reptile
H scales
I trait
J species
K extinct
L threatened
M fossil
N endangered

Harcourt

Use with pages A40–A81.

Name _____

Date _____

Write Bird-Watching Field Notes

Informative Writing—Description

Imagine you are a bird-watcher who has sighted a new kind of bird. Draw a picture of the bird. Think of a name for the bird. Write a set of field notes describing the bird's traits. Use the outline below to help you plan your writing.

Drawing of Bird

Field Notes

Name of Bird: _____

Habitat: _____

Traits

Size: _____

Color: _____

Beak Shape: _____

Foot Shape: _____

Where It Nests: _____

Harcourt

Chapter 1 • Graphic Organizer for Chapter Concepts

Where Living Things Are Found

LESSON 1
WHAT ARE ECOSYSTEMS?

1. The environment
the living and nonliving things that surround a specific living thing

2. A population
a group of the same type of living thing living in the same place at the same time

3. A community
all the populations living in an ecosystem.

4. A habitat
the home of a population

LESSON 2
WHAT ARE FOREST ECOSYSTEMS?

1. A deciduous forest
has trees that shed their leaves every year.

2. A tropical rain forest
grows in warm, rainy places.

3. A coastal forest
is like a tropical rain forest but is damp and cool.

4. A coniferous forest
has trees with needlelike leaves that stay green all year.

LESSON 3
WHAT IS A DESERT ECOSYSTEM?

Hot and cold deserts have little rain. Plants and animals must have parts that help them save water and keep cool.

LESSON 4
WHAT IS A GRASSLAND ECOSYSTEM?

1. Rainfall
is not high enough for most trees to grow but too high for a desert to form.

2. Temperature
is high in summer and low in winter.

LESSON 5
WHAT ARE WATER ECOSYSTEMS?

1. Freshwater ecosystems
include lakes, rivers, streams, ponds, and some marshes. Some freshwater ecosystems have flowing water. Others have standing water.

2. Saltwater ecosystems
include oceans, seas, marshes, tide pool, and some lakes. The water is salty. Plants and animals with adaptions for salt live in these ecosystems.

Harcourt

Observing an Environment

Materials

wire clothes hanger

Activity Procedure

1 Bend your hanger to make a square. Go outside and place the hanger on the ground. Inside this square is the environment you will **observe**.

2 Make a list of all the things you **observe** below. Next to each thing on your list, **record** whether it is living or nonliving. Write *L* for living and *N* for nonliving.

3 Ask a classmate to share his or her list with you. **Compare** the environments each of you observed.

4 Choose a living thing you **observed** in your hanger environment. Talk with a classmate about which things in the environment help the living thing survive.

_____   _____

_____   _____

_____   _____

_____   _____

_____   _____

_____   _____

Harcourt

Name _____

Draw Conclusions

1. Describe the environment you **observed.** Answers depend on the
environment observed. Students should mention both living and
nonliving things.

_____

_____

_____

2. How can you use **observation** to find out how an animal lives?
Answers should include that observing an animal's environment can
tell you what the animal eats and what kind of shelter it may have.

_____

_____

_____

3. Scientists at Work Scientists learn by **observing** and by **gathering data.**
They also learn from the data gathered by others. What did you learn
about an environment from your classmate's data?
Answers should include that sharing observations with others is
helpful in learning new information.

_____

_____

_____

Investigate Further Observe a sample of soil in which an earthworm lives.
Describe the environment. **Predict** what would happen if all the
earthworms disappeared. _____

_____

_____

_____

Harcourt

Name _____

Date _____

Observing and Gathering Data

During experiments, you collect measurements like times and temperatures. At the end of the experiment, you arrange these measurements to make it easier to interpret the data.

Think About Observing and Gathering Data

Three third-grade classes in three different schools did a joint bug-observing project. Each class observed an environment once a week for four weeks. The classes gathered data and recorded their observations. Class 1 observed ants and an anthill on the playground next to the kindergarten sandbox. The students used a hand lens to observe the ants. Class 2 observed yellow banana slugs under a barrel in the woods next to their school. Class 3 found a caterpillar on a tree and observed it. Fill in the chart below with the classes' observations.

	Environment	Nonliving Things	Living Things
Class 1	the playground	anthill, sandbox	ants
Class 2	the woods	barrel	slugs
Class 3	a tree		caterpillar

1. What do you think you can learn about a living thing by observing it?

   You may learn where it lives, what it eats, or how it moves.

2. Why do you think Class 1 used a hand lens to observe the ants?

   Because ants are very small; the hand lens will let you see more

   details of the ants.

Harcourt

Use with page B5.

Name _____

Date _____

Predict Possible Future Outcomes

The Flood

Jason and his family live on a small street. Many families and their pets live in homes on the street. A stream flows behind their houses. Animals such as ducks, fish, frogs, and insects make their homes in and near the stream. Deer often come to drink the water from the stream and eat the berries from the plants that grow there. Birds make nests in the tall trees. One spring it rained so much that the water in the stream spilled over its banks and flooded the street, the homes, and the entire area near the stream. The flood remained for many days before the water returned to its normal level.

Write a paragraph below that predicts how all the living things might have been affected by the flood.

Accept all reasonable responses. Paragraphs should include that the homes of many animals may have been destroyed because of the floodwaters. Jason and his family as well as other families and their pets may have had to leave their homes and find temporary shelter. Their homes may have been ruined. The deer could not have drunk from the stream or eaten the berries from the plants because the plants were underwater. The homes of the birds remained intact, but the birds may have had difficulty finding food. Once the floodwaters receded, plants may have regrown and animals may have rebuilt their homes as long as they were able to get what they needed to live.

Harcourt

What Are Ecosystems?

Lesson Concept

The living and nonliving things that interact and affect each other form an ecosystem.

Vocabulary

environment (B6)   **ecosystem** (B7)   **population** (B7)

community (B7)   **habitat** (B7)

Underline the best answer.

1. A large number of frogs are spotted in a pond. All the frogs in the ecosystem are ____.

   A a habitat   **B** an ecosystem   **C** a population

2. Other living things live in the pond. All the living things in the ecosystem are ____.

   A a habitat   **B** an environment   **C** a community

3. A ____ provides for the needs of the groups living in the pond.

   A population   **B** habitat   **C** ecosystem

4. Draw an ecosystem in the aquarium below. Make a habitat of water, rocks, and plants. Add a population of fish.

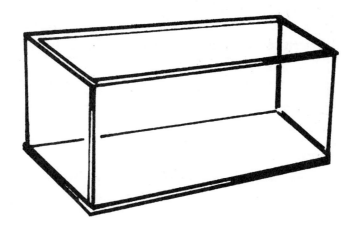

Harcourt

Variety in Forests

Materials

 tray of beans, labeled "Tray 1"

 tray of beans, labeled "Tray 2"

 2 paper cups

Activity Procedure

1 Tray 1 stands for the trees in a tropical rain forest. Tray 2 stands for the trees in a deciduous forest. Each kind of bean stands for a different kind of tree.

2 Scoop a cupful of beans from each tray. Carefully pour each cup of beans into its own pile.

3 Work with a partner. One partner should work with the beans from Tray 1. The other partner should work with the beans from Tray 2.

4 Sort the beans into groups so that each group contains only one kind of bean.

5 **Record** a description of each type of bean in the data table below. Count the number of beans in each small pile. Record these numbers in the data table.

Tropical Rain Forest (Tray 1)		Deciduous Forest (Tray 2)	
Kind of Bean	**Number of Beans**	**Kind of Bean**	**Number of Beans**

Name _____

Draw Conclusions

1. How many kinds of "trees" were in each "forest"? _The answers will_
depend on how many beans and how many types of beans the
student scoops up. The rain forest should have more kinds of trees
than the deciduous forest.

2. Which forest had the most trees of one kind? Why do you think this
was so? _The deciduous forest had the greatest number of trees of the_
same kind. The reason is that there are fewer kinds of trees so there
is a greater chance (given the same number of trees) that there
would be more of one type of tree in the deciduous forest.

3. **Scientists at Work** Scientists learn by **gathering, recording,** and
interpreting data. What did you learn from your data about variety
in forests? _The data showed that each type of forest had several_
different kinds of trees. There were fewer numbers of more types of
trees in the rain forest; there were more trees of fewer types in the
deciduous forest.

Investigate Further Suppose you want to find out what kinds of trees are
most common in your community. Explain how you could **use numbers** to

find out. _____

_____

_____

Harcourt

Name _____

Date _____

Use Numbers

Using numbers is one way to gather information and record data from an investigation. You can draw a conclusion based on the data you collect.

Think About Using Numbers

Roger lives on a farm. He writes to his pen pal, Teresa, "Our apple trees are doing well this year. We are taking lots of apples to the farmers' market every Tuesday." Teresa writes back, "I live in the city. I've never ever seen an apple tree. How many apples do you take to the market on one day?" Roger goes out into the barn. He sees apples in boxes, piled high. He doesn't want to count every one. He reads the side of one of the boxes and sees that there are 50 apples in each box. He writes that number in his notebook. He counts the boxes. There are 10. Roger writes to Teresa, "We are taking 500 apples to the market this week!"

Apples: 50 in each box
Boxes: 10

1. Why do you think Roger didn't want to count each apple? It would take too long, and the apples were already packed in boxes.

2. What did Roger want to investigate? how many apples were being taken to market

3. What data did Roger gather and record? how many apples were in each box and how many boxes there were in total

4. What conclusion did Roger come to? There were 500 apples total.

5. How do you think Roger used numbers to come to this conclusion? He could have either added or multiplied.

Use with page B13.

Harcourt

Name _____

Date _____

 **Investigate Log**

Make a Desert Ecosystem

Materials

shoe box

plastic wrap

sandy soil

2 or 3 desert plants

small rocks

Activity Procedure

1 **Make a model** of a desert ecosystem. Start by lining the shoe box with plastic wrap. Place sandy soil in the shoe box. Make sure the soil is deep enough for the plants.

2 Place the plants in the soil, and place the rocks around them. Lightly sprinkle the soil with water.

3 Place your desert ecosystem in a sunny location.

4 Every two or three days, use your finger to **observe** how dry the soil is. If the soil is *very* dry, add a small amount of water. If the soil is damp, do not add water. Be careful not to water the plants too much.

5 Continue to **observe** and care for your desert ecosystem. **Record** what you observe.

My Observations: _____

_____

_____

_____

Name _____

Draw Conclusions

1. What kind of environment does your desert ecosystem model?
The ecosystem models a desert environment that is dry, warm,
and sunny.
_____

2. How does **making a model** help you learn about a desert?
Students who live far from a desert may say that making and
observing a model of a desert allows them to observe firsthand.

3. **Scientists at Work** Scientists often learn by **making models**. What other
types of ecosystems can you make models of? Answers will depend
on the ecosystem chosen. All ecosystems can be modeled.

Investigate Further How would getting rain every day change a desert
ecosystem? **Plan an experiment** in which you could **use a model** to find out.
Students will likely suggest watering their ecosystem daily and
making observations over time to see the changes this added rainfall
would make.

Harcourt

Name _____

Date _____

Make a Model

Sometimes you may want to observe something that is very large.
You can make a small model and observe the model instead.

Think About Making a Model

You live in a climate that is hot and dry in the summer and cold and rainy
in the winter. Suppose you make a model of a desert ecosystem in the backyard of your home. You make it during the hottest part of the summer. You
plant some desert plants in sandy soil. Each day the blazing sun shines on your
ecosystem. You give the plants a few drops of water once a week. The plants
grow well. Then, when the summer is over, your ecosystem begins to change.

1. What is the purpose of a model? Student's answer should show an
understanding that a model helps you learn about something when
observing the real thing would be difficult.

2. What does this model teach you? Desert plants grow well in an
ecosystem that is hot, dry, and sandy and has lots of sun.

3. What do you think will happen to your model at the end of the summer?
Answers may include these ideas: The environment will change; the
conditions of a desert ecosystem will no longer be there; there
won't be enough sun; there will be too much water; it won't be a
desert ecosystem anymore.

4. Draw a picture of the backyard desert ecosystem.

Harcourt

Name _____

Date _____

Use Graphic Sources for Information

Desert Animals

Use the pictures to help you answer the questions.

1. How does the snake keep cool in the hot desert?

from the shade provided by the rock
_____

2. How does the bird get water?

from the water stored in the cactus plant
_____

3. How does the lizard keep warm at night?

from the rocks that were heated during the day
_____

4. Name one animal that is active during the night.

bat or squirrel
_____

Harcourt

Use with page B23.

Name _____

Date _____

What Is a Desert Ecosystem?

A desert is an ecosystem found in areas that get very little rainfall.

Vocabulary

desert (B22)

Underline the best answer.

1. Hot deserts can have temperatures of over ____ during the day.

A 23°C (about 73° F)　　　　　**B** 43°C (about 110° F)

2. The Taklimakan desert in China has ____ in the winter.

A freezing temperatures　　　　**B** notably high
and blizzards　　　　　　　　　　　temperatures

3. The barrel cactus has parts that allow it to live in hot deserts. The barrel
cactus does NOT have ____.

A a thick skin　　**B** very deep　　**C** a thick stem　　**D** very shallow
roots　　　　　　　　　　　　　　　　　　roots

4. Desert animals get most of their water from eating plants or ____.

A fruits　　　　　**B** vegetables　　**C** other animals　**D** nuts

5. You want to observe rabbits in the desert. Should you look for them

during the day or during the night? Explain. Look for them during the

night. In the desert, rabbits are active at night, when it is cooler.

_____

Harcourt

Name _____

Date _____

Grass Roots

Materials

trowel   paper   hand lens

Activity Procedure

1. **CAUTION** **Make sure you have permission to dig in the spot you choose.** Dig out a small clump of grass, about the size of your palm. Be sure to include the roots. (Picture A)

2. Hold up the clump of grass. **Observe** what happens to the soil around the roots. Gently shake the grass, and again **observe** the soil around the roots.

3. Carefully remove the soil from the roots, and separate one grass plant from the rest.

4. Put the grass plant on a clean sheet of paper. **Observe** it with the hand lens. The leaves of a grass plant are called blades. Notice how the roots and blades are shaped. (Picture B)

5. Draw your grass plant. Label the roots and blades.

Harcourt

Name _____

Draw Conclusions

1. Describe the roots of grass plants. How might they help hold soil in place?

The roots of grass plants are short and tangled, with many branches.

(Scientists call these fibrous root systems.) This tangle of roots might

help hold soil in place.

2. Think about the leaves of other plants. How do grass blades **compare** with the leaves of other plants?

Grass leaves are very long and narrow compared with most other

plants.

_____

3. Scientists at Work Scientists make inferences about plants by closely **observing** them. The blades of grass plants do not lose much water to the air around them. Grass roots can absorb water from large areas of soil. From these facts, **infer** the kinds of places in which many grasses live.

Grasses are adapted to live in somewhat dry areas.

_____

_____

Investigate Further Take a walk in the neighborhood. Look for places where the soil has been washed away. **Observe** the slope of the land and the plants growing in those places. **Form a hypothesis** about how to prevent more soil from washing away. Share your hypothesis with your class.

Harcourt

Name _____

Date _____

Observe and Infer

When you **observe**, you use your senses to find out what is happening. You then can use what you have observed to **infer** an opinion or an explanation.

Think About Observing and Inferring

Suppose that you take a trip to another state. While you are there, you notice that the grass is very dry and brown. You remember that the grass where you live is soft and green.

1. What did you **observe** about the grass in the place you are visiting?

The grass is dry and brown.

2. What did you **observe** about the grass where you live?

The grass where you live is soft and green.

3. What are some possible reasons that the grass in the place you are visiting is dry and brown?

not enough rain

poor soil quality

grass not receiving enough sunlight

4. From the reasons you gave in Question 3, choose one and write a sentence stating what you have **inferred** about why the grass is dry and brown.

Possible response: The grass is dry and brown because there has

not been enough rain recently to provide the grass with the amount

of water it needs.

5. What is one way to find out whether your inference is correct?

Possible response: I could read the newspaper to see how much

rain the area has received in the recent past.

Harcourt

Use with page B27.

Name _____

Date _____

Compare and Contrast

Fish in the Water

Many different types of fish live in water. All fish have backbones. They also breathe through gills. Some fish live in freshwater areas, and others live in saltwater areas. Freshwater fish have several things in common. They usually cannot live in water that has too much salt in it. Freshwater fish absorb, or take in, large amounts of water through the linings of their bodies. Saltwater fish also have things in common with each other. Saltwater fish usually cannot live in water that is not salty. Saltwater fish lose large amounts of water through their body linings. Some fish can live in both freshwater and saltwater environments. These fish can adapt, or change, to fit the different amounts of salt in fresh water and salt water.

Use the information in the selection to compare and contrast freshwater fish, saltwater fish, and fish that can live in both environments.

1. What do freshwater fish have in common?

Freshwater fish cannot live in salt water. They absorb large amounts of water through their body linings.

2. How are saltwater fish different from freshwater fish?

Saltwater fish cannot live in fresh water. They lose large amounts of water through their body linings.

3. In what ways are freshwater and saltwater fish the same?

Both freshwater fish and saltwater fish have backbones and breathe through gills.

4. How are fish that can live in both freshwater and saltwater environments different from fish that can live only in fresh water or salt water?

They can adapt to changing salt contents.

_____

Harcourt

Grasslands

Lesson Concept

Grasslands are large areas in which there is enough water for grass to grow but not enough water to support the growth of trees.

Vocabulary

grassland (B28)

Place a check mark in front of the sentence in each pair that is a fact about grasslands.

1. ____ Grasslands have lots of grass, trees, shrubs, and wildflowers.

✓ Grasslands have lots of grass but few, if any, trees.

2. ____ Grasslands receive about as much rainfall as deserts.

✓ Grasslands receive more rainfall than deserts.

3. ✓ Grasslands are large, flat areas.

____ Grasslands are small, hilly areas.

4. ____ Grasslands are found in only a few areas of the United States and nowhere else.

✓ Grasslands are found in many places around the world.

5. ____ Grasslands are also called *mountains* or *deserts*.

✓ Grasslands are also called *pampas* or *steppes*.

6. ✓ Many different types of animals live in grasslands.

____ Very few animals live in grasslands.

7. ____ Many animals in grasslands make their homes from sticks and twigs.

✓ Many animals in grasslands make their homes in underground burrows.

Harcourt

Name _____

Date _____

Make a Freshwater Ecosystem

Materials

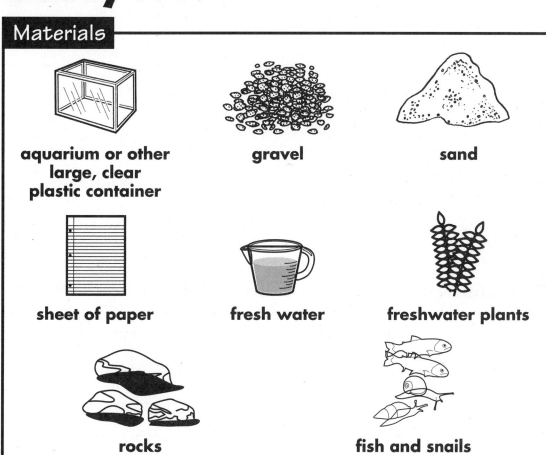

aquarium or other large, clear plastic container

gravel

sand

sheet of paper

fresh water

freshwater plants

rocks

fish and snails

Activity Procedure

1. Put a layer of gravel at the bottom of the tank. Add a layer of sand on top of the gravel.

2. Set the aquarium in a place where it isn't too sunny. Place a sheet of paper over the sand. Slowly add the water to the tank. Make sure you pour the water onto the paper so the sand will stay in place.

3. Remove the paper, and put the plants and rocks into the tank. Let the tank sit for about one week. After one week, add the fish and snails.

4. **Observe** and care for your freshwater ecosystem.

Harcourt

Use with pages B32–B33.   **(page 1 of 2)**

Draw Conclusions

1. What are some things you **observed** in your freshwater ecosystem?

Answers may include that the numbers of living things have
changed. For example, the snail population may have increased or
some plants may have died.

_____

2. Why do you think you waited to add the fish to the tank?

Waiting a week to add the fish gave the plants time to add oxygen to
the water. Some students may note that the water may contain
harmful chemicals, such as chlorine, which are removed after the
water sits for a time. Accept all reasonable answers.

_____

3. Scientists at Work Scientists often **make a model** of an ecosystem so they can **observe** it in a laboratory. How did making a model help you observe a freshwater ecosystem? How is your model different from a real pond?

Students should understand that it is often difficult to observe an
ecosystem in nature. By building a model, you can keep a close
watch on the interactions.

_____

Investigate Further What other kinds of plants and animals might live in a freshwater ecosystem? To find out, visit a pet shop that sells fish. Make a list of the freshwater plants and animals you find there. _____

_____

_____

_____

_____

Harcourt

Name _____

Date _____

Make a Model

You can make a model to observe something that would be difficult to observe in the classroom. When you make a model, you have to be careful, or your model won't work.

Think About Making a Model

Jeff made a model of a freshwater ecosystem. He put a layer of gravel on the bottom of a large, clear plastic container. He added a layer of sand. He poured water into the tank. The sand would not stay in place. It clouded the water. He had to start again. He put paper over the sand and poured the water in. He set his plants and rocks on top of the paper. When he saw what he had done, he had to take the plants and rocks out again. He took the paper off. Then he put the plants and rocks into the tank. He added the fish and snails right away. The fish did not look well. He took them out and put them back in his other aquarium. He let the water sit for a week. He added the fish and snails. They did well.

1. What mistakes did Jeff make in his model of a freshwater ecosystem?

   He did not put paper over the sand; the sand clouded the water.

   He put the plants and rocks on top of the paper; he forgot to remove

   the paper. He put the fish in too soon.

2. Infer why the fish and snails did not do well when Jeff put them in the
   tank without waiting a week. Possible answers: something was wrong

   with the water, the water would be clear and settled after a week, or

   the plants had not had time to put oxygen into the water.

3. Write the correct steps for making a model of a freshwater ecosystem.

   A. Put a layer of gravel on the bottom of a large, clear plastic

   container. B. Add a layer of sand. C. Put paper over the sand,

   then pour in water. D. Take the paper off, and then put plants and

   rocks into the tank. E. Wait one week, and then add fish and snails.

Harcourt

WB76 Work

Name _____

Date _____

Compare and Contrast

Water Ecosystems

freshwater	saltwater	ocean	lake	salt
tide pool	barnacles	American egret		river

Fill in the blanks using the words above.

In a _freshwater_ ecosystem, the water contains very little salt. In a _saltwater_ ecosystem, the water has a lot of _salt_. An example of a saltwater ecosystem is an _ocean_. An example of a freshwater ecosystem is a _river_. A _tide pool_ is a saltwater ecosystem that forms at an ocean shoreline. _Barnacles_ are small animals that live there. A _lake_ is a freshwater ecosystem that is usually larger and deeper than a pond. An _American egret_ is a wading bird that might make its home near a pond.

Write a sentence that tells how freshwater and saltwater ecosystems are similar. _Possible response: Both freshwater and saltwater ecosystems contain living things._

Harcourt

Use with page B38.

Name _____

Date _____

What Are Water Ecosystems?

Lesson Concept

Water ecosystems may have salt water or fresh water.

Vocabulary

salt water (B26)   **fresh water** (B26)

Underline the best answer.

1. You go on a field trip to the aquarium. It is near the ocean. You see a display of a kelp forest. It is 10 meters (about 30 ft) deep. Which ecosystem are you looking at?

   A freshwater   **B** saltwater

2. A beach is right outside the aquarium. Shallow salt water collects in the middle of some big rocks on the beach. The sun warms the water. Many plants and animals live in the warm, shallow water. What is the correct name for this area?

   A pond   **B** river   **C** tide pool   **D** kelp forest

3. At the aquarium, you see a movie about ecosystems. People are swimming. When the people finish swimming, you see how still the water is. You see turtles crawling at the edge of the water. What kind

   of ecosystem is this? How do you know? __It is a freshwater ecosystem.__

   __You know because the water is still, which means it is in a lake.__

   __A lake is a freshwater ecosystem.__

Harcourt

Recognize Vocabulary

In the space provided, write the letter of the term in Column B
that best fits the definition in Column A. Use each term only once.

Column A

_____ **1.** a forest that contains mostly evergreens

_____ **2.** an ecosystem found in areas that get very little rainfall

_____ **3.** water that has lots of salt in it

_____ **4.** an area in which the main plants are trees

_____ **5.** everything around a living thing

_____ **6.** provides a population with all its needs

_____ **7.** a forest mostly made up of trees that drop their leaves each fall

_____ **8.** water that has very little salt in it

_____ **9.** a forest that grows in places that are hot and wet all year

_____ **10.** living and nonliving things interacting in an environment

_____ **11.** a group of the same kind of living things that live in the same place at the same time

_____ **12.** a forest that grows where it does not get too warm or too cold and where there is a lot of rain

_____ **13.** all the populations that live in an ecosystem

Column B

A fresh water

B coniferous forest

C desert

D environment

E ecosystem

F tropical rain forest

G coastal forest

H salt water

I forest

J population

K community

L deciduous forest

M habitat

Harcourt

Name _____

Date _____

Write a Web Page

Persuasive Writing–Request

Imagine that you work for a group that wants to protect desert ecosystems. Write three paragraphs for the group's Web page. Tell readers about the animals and plants that live in the desert. Ask people not to do things that can damage the desert ecosystem. Use the outline below to help you plan your Web page.

Paragraph 1
Animals and plants that live in the desert

Paragraph 2
Things that can damage the desert ecosystem

Paragraph 3
Reasons people should not damage the desert ecosystem

Harcourt

Chapter 2 • Graphic Organizer for Chapter Concepts

Living Things Depend on One Another

LESSON 1   HOW DO LIVING THINGS GET FOOD?

They _____ with their environment to get _____ what they need .

interact

Producers _____ interact with sunlight, air, and water to make their own food.

Consumers   Animals are _____ . They eat other living things.

Decomposers _____ eat other living things that have died.

LESSON 2   MODELS OF THESE INTERACTIONS ARE

Food chains _____ , which show how food and energy move from one living thing to another.

Energy pyramid _____ , which shows how energy decreases at each level of the food chain.

LESSON 3   WHICH IN TURN LEAD TO FOOD WEBS

A food web is made of _____ food chains that overlap and link together .

Members of the Food Web Are

Predators _____ , which are animals that hunt and eat other animals.

Prey _____ , which are animals that are hunted and used as food.

Plants _____

Harcourt

Name _____

Date _____

Animal Teeth

Materials

blank index cards

books about animals

Activity Procedure

1. **Observe** the pictures of the animals. Look closely at the shape of each animal's teeth.

2. Use one index card for each animal. **Record** the animal's name, and draw the shape of its teeth.

3. With a partner, make a list of words that describe the teeth. **Record** these words next to the drawings on the index cards.

4. Think about the things each animal eats. Use books about animals if you need help. On the back of each index card, make a list of the things the animal eats.

Harcourt

Name _____

Draw Conclusions

1. Which animals might use their teeth to catch other animals? Which animals might use their teeth to eat plants? Explain.

Students should identify the animals with sharp front teeth as those
that catch and eat other animals. Those with flatter teeth should be
identified as those that eat mainly plants.

2. Some animals use their teeth to help them do other things, too. **Observe** the beaver's teeth. How do its teeth help it cut down trees?

The beaver's front teeth are long and sharp. They act as chisels,
cutting away at the tree's trunk. The beaver uses the trees to build
its dam and lodge.

3. **Scientists at Work** Scientists learn by **observing**. Scientists can learn about how animals use their teeth by watching how and what the animals eat. From what you observed in this investigation, what can you **infer**

about the shapes of animals' teeth? The shape of an animal's teeth
matches the food it eats. Some animals use sharp teeth to help
them catch and eat meat. Other animals have flat teeth to help
them chew plants.

Harcourt

Observe and Infer

When you observe, you use your senses. When you infer, you form an opinion based on what you have observed.

Think About Observing and Inferring

Your class goes on a field trip to a natural history museum. You see a display of wolves in their natural habitat. You observe that these animals have very sharp front teeth. In another display you see pictures of a dairy farm. You learn that cows have flat, grinding teeth. The final display shows the 32 teeth of an adult person. You learn that the front teeth are for cutting food, and the teeth next to them are sharp for ripping. The teeth way in the back have a fairly flat surface for grinding food.

1. Think about the cow's teeth. What inference can you make about what cows eat? Cows probably eat plants of some kind; cows may eat grass; cows may eat grains; cows probably don't eat meat, because meat needs to be torn by sharp teeth.

2. What inference could you make about the purpose of a person's front teeth? The front teeth are for biting or cutting food.

3. From your observations of animal teeth, make up an imaginary animal. Let it be an animal that eats only plants. Draw a picture showing the teeth of the animal. Explain what the animal eats. The drawing should feature flat, grinding teeth. Explanations should indicate that the animal is a plant- or grain-eater.

Harcourt

Name _____

Date _____

Identify Cause and Effect

Read the sentences below. In each sentence, underline the cause and circle the effect.

1. A carrot plant uses <u>energy from the sun</u> to (make its own food.)

2. As an <u>earthworm feeds,</u> it (helps clean the environment.)

3. A <u>hungry rabbit</u> (eats) a carrot for energy.

Read the paragraph, looking for causes and effects. Then finish the chart with three causes and effects found in the paragraph.

   A farmer planted a crop of corn. After getting a lot of sunlight and water, the corn plants grew very tall. Just before harvest, hungry crows flew into the field and started eating the corn. The farmer did not want the crows in his field because he was afraid they would ruin his crop. The farmer made two large scarecrows and placed them in the middle of the cornfield. The crows stopped coming to eat the corn. The farmer harvested the corn crop and sold most of the corn by the bushel. The farmer used the rest of the corn to feed his family.

Cause	Effect
a lot of sunlight and water	corn plants grew
two large scarecrows	crows stopped eating corn
farmer harvested a crop	farmer was able to sell corn and use it to feed his family

Harcourt

Use with page B52.

How Do Animals Get Food?

Lesson Concept

Plants and animals depend on their environment and on one another to get the food they need.

Vocabulary

interact (B50)   **herbivore** (B51)   **producer** (B51)
consumer (B51)   **carnivore** (B52)   **decomposer** (B52)
                      omnivore (B52)

As you read the summary, fill in each blank with a vocabulary term from above. Answer the questions that follow.

Plants and animals work together, or _____ with the

environment to get what they need. Plants are _____.

They make their own food. Animals are _____. They

must eat plants or other animals. A _____ is a living
thing that breaks down once-living things for food.

Make a check mark in front of the statements that agree with your reading.

_____ All living things need food.

_____ Plants interact with sunlight, air, and water to make food.

_____ Animals that hunt and kill their food have body parts that help
them get their food.

_____ Omnivores eat both plants and animals.

_____ Carnivores eat plants.

_____ Herbivores eat animals.

Use with page B53.

Harcourt

Name _____

Date _____

Make a Food-Chain Model

Materials

index cards

4 pieces of yarn or string

marker

tape

Activity Procedure

1. In the bottom right-hand corners, number the index cards 1 through 5.

2. On Card 1, draw and label grass. On Card 2, draw and label a cricket. On Card 3, draw and label a frog. On Card 4, draw and label a snake. On Card 5, draw and label a hawk.

3. Order the cards in a line with Card 1 first and Card 5 last. Use yarn and tape to connect the cards.

4. Stretch the connected cards out on a table. The cards form a model called a food chain.

5. Discuss with a classmate how each living thing in the food chain gets its food. Tell which things in your model show producers. Tell which things show consumers.

Harcourt

Name _____

Draw Conclusions

1. In your model, which living thing is last in the food chain? Why do you think it is in this place? _The hawk is at the top of the food chain_ _because it eats animals that eat other animals._

2. In which part of the food chain is the producer found? Why do you think it is there? _The producer (grass) is found at the bottom of the_ _food chain. It supplies energy for the rest of the living things_ _in the chain._

3. **Scientists at Work** Scientists **use models** to help them study things in nature. How does using a model of a food chain help you understand living things and the food they eat? _The model makes it easier_ _to see how living things get food without observing all of them in the_ _wild. Using the model makes the relationships between producers_ _and different types of consumers clearer._

Harcourt

Name _____

Date _____

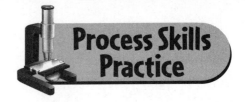

Make a Model

Using a model helps you learn about something you cannot observe in real life.

Think About Making a Model

You can make a model of a food chain by using the chart below. Write the names of these animals and plants in the correct columns: a whale; a pelican, which is a bird that eats fish; a small fish; and an ocean plantlike living thing called algae. Fill in the chart as you answer the questions.

Producers	Consumers	Food Chain
algae	whale	1. whale and pelican
	pelican	2. fish
	small fish	3. algae

Fill in the chart as you answer the questions.

1. What would you list in the *Consumers* column? whale, pelican, and small fish

2. What is a consumer? An animal is a consumer; a consumer cannot make its own food; a consumer is a living thing that eats other living things as food.

3. What would you list in the *Producers* column? algae

4. What is a producer? A living thing that makes its own food; plants are producers.

5. In the *Food Chain* column, list the four living things from the paragraph. Write the number *1* next to the living thing or things at the top of the food chain. Number the other living things to show their order in the food chain.

Harcourt

Name _____

Date _____

Arrange Events in Sequence

These sentences are out of order. Reorder the sentences to write a paragraph describing the food chain.

A zebra is a consumer that eats grass.

The stored food contains energy.

As the zebra eats the grass, it takes in energy.

The plants make and store their own food.

All plants are producers.

A lion is also a consumer, eating zebras for energy.

All plants are producers. The plants make and store their own food.

The stored food contains energy. A zebra is a consumer that eats

grass. As the zebra eats the grass, it takes in energy. A lion is also a

consumer, eating zebras for energy.

_____

_____

_____

_____

Harcourt

Use with page B57.

Concept Review

What Are Food Chains?

Lesson Concept

A food chain is the path of food in an ecosystem from one living thing to another.

Vocabulary

food chain (B56)   **energy pyramid** (B58)

Read the summary, and fill in the blanks with vocabulary terms from above.

All living things need energy to live. Living things get their energy from food. Producers get energy from sunlight and store energy in the food they make. Animals cannot make their own food, so they eat other living things.

A _____food chain_____ shows how energy moves through the

environment. An _____energy pyramid_____ is a model that shows how the amount of energy in an ecosystem goes down for each higher animal in the food chain.

1. Underline the correct answer. A rabbit nibbles on grass. A bird eats a worm. Both animals are ____, which get energy from the food they eat.

consumers   producers   observers   meat-eaters

2. Put the stages of this food chain in the correct order by numbering each living thing with a 1, 2, 3, or 4, beginning with the blades of grass.

____3____   ____1____   ____2____   ____4____

3. Suppose you have a peanut butter and jelly sandwich for lunch. Do the fillings of your sandwich come from producers or consumers?

producers _____

Harcourt

Name _____

Date _____

Make a Food Web

Materials

index cards, cut into fourths

poster board

tape or glue

crayons

Activity Procedure

1 Write the name of each living thing from the chart on its own card.

2 Glue the cards onto a sheet of poster board so they form a circle. Leave room for writing.

3 Look at the chart again. List two different food chains you could make.

4 Draw arrows between the parts of each food chain. Use a different color for each food chain. You have now made a food web.

5 **Observe** your model to see how the food chains overlap. What other living things could you add to your food web?

Harcourt

Living Thing	What It Eats
clover	uses the sun to make its own food
grasshopper	clover
frog	grasshopper
snake	frog, mouse
owl	snake
mouse	clover

Draw Conclusions

1. What is the producer in this food web? clover _____

2. What does your food web tell you about producers and consumers?

Producers provide food for several types of consumers. Some

consumers may be eaten by several other consumers.

3. **Scientists at Work** Scientists sometimes **make models** to help them learn about things. How did drawing a food web help you learn about animals

in a real ecosystem? The model food web showed that an ecosystem

can have more than one food chain.

_____

Investigate Further Cut out magazine pictures of different plants and animals. Work with a partner to make a food web that includes these plants and animals.

Harcourt

Use a Model

When you make a model, you can learn about something that is hard to observe, such as a real-life food web.

Think About Using a Model

Chris visited the wetland near her house. She wrote down some of the things she saw. Some fish splashed in the stream. Caterpillars in the trees munched on new leaves. One fell into the water and was eaten by a fish. A bird swooped down into the water and came out again with a fish in its beak. Grubs crawled on the tree, chewing at the tree's bark. Another bird appeared and picked up one of the grubs in its beak. Chris made drawings of each of the things she saw. She cut out her drawings and glued them to a piece of cardboard. She drew arrows to connect the living things. Now she had a food web. After that, Chris sat down and ate a fish sandwich for lunch. Then she drew a picture of herself and added it to the food web.

1. What is the producer in this food web? _the leaves_____

2. What are the consumers in this food web? _Chris, fish, bird, grubs, and_
   _caterpillar_____

3. List the different food chains in the food web. _leaves → caterpillar →_
   fish → Chris; tree bark → grubs → bird; leaves → caterpillar →
   fish → bird

4. Why did Chris put herself on the food web? _because the fish she ate_
   _was part of a food chain_____

5. Make a food web of the different food chains you are a part of.

Harcourt

Name _____

Date _____

Use Graphic Sources for Information

Look at the food web for this freshwater ecosystem. Finish the chart showing the food source or sources for each living thing.

Living Thing	Food Source
plants	energy from the sun; make their own food
fish	plants
insects	plants
duck	plants, insects
loon	plants, fish
chipmunk	grass
grass	energy from the sun; makes its own food
hawk	duck, loon, chipmunk

Harcourt

Name _____

Date _____

What Are Food Webs?

Lesson Concept

A food web is a model that shows how food chains overlap and link together.

Vocabulary

food web (B54) **predator** (B54) **prey** (B54)

Look at the food web. Answer the questions that follow.

1. What is a predator? _an animal that hunts other animals for food_

2. Which of the animals on the food web are predators?
   fish, bird, frog, and rat

3. What is prey? _an animal that is hunted_

4. Which of the animals are prey? _fish, frog, grasshopper, and snail_

5. How can an animal, like the frog, be both predator and prey?
   If the frog eats the grasshopper, the frog is the predator; if the bird
   eats the frog, the frog is prey.

Harcourt

Name _____

Date _____

Recognize Vocabulary

Use the terms below to complete each sentence. The capital
letters will spell a hidden word. Unscramble the capital letters
to spell out the hidden word.

decompoSer	energy pyraMid	foOd chain
food wEb	conSumer	preY
produCer	prEdator	interacT

1. An animal that hunts another animal is called a _predator_____.

2. A model that shows how energy is lost for each higher animal in a food
chain is called an _energy pyramid_____.

3. The path of food from one living thing to another is a
_food chain_____.

4. An animal that is hunted is called _prey_____.

5. Overlapping food chains are called a _food web_____.

6. A living thing that breaks down the wastes of another living thing is a
_decomposer_____.

7. When plants and animals work together, they _interact_____.

8. A living thing that eats other living things is a _consumer_____.

9. A living thing that makes its own food is a _producer_____.

Hidden Word: All plants and animals interact together to form an

emoyestsc. _ecosystem_____

Harcourt

Name _____

Date _____

Explain an Energy Pyramid

Informative Writing–Explanation

Choose one ecosystem. Write a paragraph that explains the energy pyramid for that ecosystem. To help you gather your ideas, draw and label the energy pyramid below for your ecosystem.

Ecosystem _____

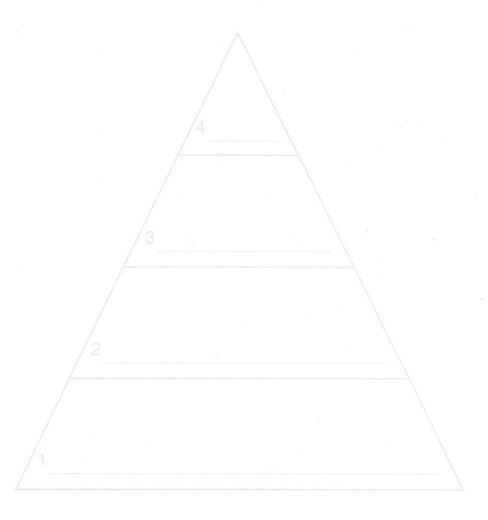

Harcourt

Chapter 1 • Graphic Organizer for Chapter Concepts

Minerals, Rocks, and Fossils

LESSON 1
MINERALS AND ROCKS

Mineral Properties

1. hardness _____

2. shape _____

3. color _____

Mineral Uses

4. season food _____

5. in body _____

6. jewelry _____

7. manufacturing _____

Rocks

8. made of minerals _____

LESSON 2
HOW ROCKS FORM

Three Kinds of Rocks

1. igneous _____

2. sedimentary _____

3. metamorphic _____

**How Rocks Change
in the Rock Cycle**

4. heat _____

5. pressure _____

6. erosion and deposition _____

Uses of Rocks

7. building materials _____

8. computer chips _____

9. jewelry _____

LESSON 3
FOSSILS

Types of Fossils

1. bones _____

2. molds _____

3. casts _____

4. imprints _____

What Fossils Show

5. life has changed over time _____

Name _____

Date _____

Investigate Log

Testing Minerals

Minerals labeled A through G

Activity Procedure

1 Use the chart below.

2 A harder mineral scratches a softer mineral. Try to scratch each of the other minerals with Sample A. **Record** which minerals Sample A scratches.

3 A softer mineral is scratched by a harder mineral. Try to scratch Sample A with each of the other minerals. **Record** which minerals scratch Sample A.

4 Repeat Steps 2 and 3 for each mineral.

5 Using the information in your chart, **order** the minerals from softest to hardest. Give each mineral a number, starting with 1 for the softest mineral.

Mineral to Test	Minerals It Scratches	Minerals that Scratch It
Sample A	B, C, D, G	E, F
Sample B	D, G	A, C, E, F
Sample C	B, D, G	A, E, F
Sample D	G	A, B, C, E, F
Sample E	A, B, C, D, G	F
Sample F	A, B, C, D, E, G	none
Sample G	none	A, B, C, D, E, F

Harcourt

Name _____

Draw Conclusions

1. Which mineral was the hardest? Sample F _____

Which was the softest? Sample G _____

How do you know? The hardest mineral was able to scratch all the

other minerals. The softest mineral was scratched by all the

other minerals.

2. How did you decide the **order** of the minerals? I used the information

in my chart to order the minerals. I compared which minerals could

be scratched by which others.

3. **Scientists at Work** Scientists often put objects in **order**. How can putting minerals in order of hardness help you identify them?

Every mineral has a specific hardness. Testing for hardness can tell

you the identity of a mineral.

Investigate Further To test for hardness, scientists sometimes scratch an unknown mineral with common objects. That's because they don't always have other minerals with them. But to use common objects, scientists need to know how hard the objects are. Using the minerals from this investigation, find out the hardness of glass, a copper penny, and your fingernail. Put them in **order** with the minerals you tested.

Harcourt

Observe and Order

Think About Observing and Ordering

Stanley wants to make a display of rocks to bring to class. He goes on a rock-collecting walk. He needs to decide how to order the rocks. He observes the rocks. He sees that the rocks are different colors. There are pink, black, gray, and white rocks. Then he observes that some of the rocks are large and some are medium sized and some are small. There are also different-shaped rocks in his collection.

1. What are three observations Stanley can make about the rocks?

The rocks are different colors.

The rocks are different sizes.

The rocks are different shapes.

2. Which sense was used to make those observations? sight

3. How could Stanley order these rocks? Accept reasonable answers like smallest to largest or heaviest to lightest.

4. Draw six different-sized rocks. Label these rocks from **A** to **F**. Put them in order from smallest to largest by writing their letters on the blanks.

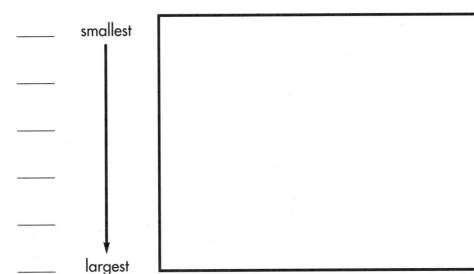

_____ smallest

_____

_____

_____

_____

_____ largest

Harcourt

Name _____

Date _____

Use Context to Determine/Confirm Word Meaning

Layers of Earth

Earth is made up of three different layers of rocks. The solid, outside layer of rock is called the <u>crust</u>. The middle layer of rock is called the <u>mantle</u>. The mantle is so hot that some of the rocks are nearly melted and are soft. The <u>core</u> is the center of Earth. Part of the core is solid and extremely hot. Another part of the core, called <u>magma</u>, is hot liquid.

Look at the underlined terms. For each term, write word clues that help define the meaning of the term.

Term	Word Clues
crust	solid outside layer rock
mantle	middle layer rock hot soft
core	extremely hot part liquid part solid
magma	hot liquid

Harcourt

What Are Minerals and Rocks?

Lesson Concept

A mineral is a solid natural material that has never been alive.
Rocks are made of minerals.

Vocabulary

rock (C8)   **core** (C8)   **mantle** (C8)   **crust** (C8)   **mineral** (C6)

Match each term with its definition on the right.

1. rock

2. crust

3. mantle

4. core

5. mineral

A hot middle layer of Earth

B a solid substance made of minerals

C the center of Earth

D the solid outside layer of Earth

E a solid natural object that has never been alive

This drawing shows Earth cut open. Label each layer with a term from the vocabulary box.

6. _____

7. _____

8. _____

Harcourt

Types of Rocks

Materials

**3 rocks labeled
I, S, and M**　　　**3 unknown rocks
labeled 1, 2, and 3**　　　**hand lens**

Activity Procedure

1 Use the chart below.

2 Rocks *I*, *S*, and *M* are three different types of rocks. Look at them with and without the hand lens. **Record** your observations in the chart.

3 Look at each of the numbered rocks with and without the hand lens. **Record** your observations in the chart.

4 **Compare** the properties of the lettered rocks with the properties of the numbered rocks. Think about how the rocks are alike and how they are different.

Rock	Observations
I	
S	
M	
1	
2	
3	

Harcourt

Name _____

Draw Conclusions

1. What properties did you use to **compare** the rocks?

Answers might include color, patterns such as specks or stripes in _the rock, shininess, and heaviness._ _____

_____

2. Which numbered rock is most like Rock I? _Rock 1_ _____

Explain your answer. _____

_____

Which numbered rock is most like Rock S? _Rock 3_ _____

Explain your answer. _____

_____

Which numbered rock is most like Rock M? _Rock 2_ _____

Explain your answer. _____

_____

3. Scientists at Work Scientists learn about new objects when they **compare** them with objects they have already studied. What did you learn about the rocks when you compared them?

_____

_____

Investigate Further Look near your school or home for small rocks. **Compare** them with Rocks *I*, *S* and *M*. Try to **classify** the rocks as *I*, *S*, or *M*.

Harcourt

Compare and Observe

Think About Comparing and Observing

Diego's class went to a natural history museum to see an exhibition of rocks. The next day his teacher gave them a worksheet to fill out.

Rock 1   **Rock 2**   **Rock 3**   **Rock 4**

1. Look at the four rocks above. Name three properties of the rocks you can observe. color, size, and shape _____

2. Which of the two rocks are similar? Rock ____1____ and Rock ____3____

3. Compare the two rocks. Which two properties are the same?
   size and shape _____

4. Compare Rock 1 and Rock 2. In what ways are they different from each other?
   Rock 2 is darker. Rock 1 is square, and Rock 2 is round.
   Rock 1 is large, and Rock 2 is small.

   _____

5. Why is it important to make good observations before you compare?
   You must know what properties an object has before you can find
   out if another object has or doesn't have the same properties.

   _____

Harcourt

Name _____

Date _____

Arrange Events in Sequence

The sentences below are not in order. Rewrite the sentences in a paragraph that describes how some sedimentary rocks are formed.

Sediment then builds up in layers at the bottom of rivers, lakes, seas, and oceans.

Rivers carry sediment, or pieces of rocks and soil.

These layers are pressed and stuck together to form sedimentary rocks.

When a river slows down, it drops the sediment.

How Sedimentary Rocks Form

Rivers carry sediment, or pieces of rocks and soil. When a river slows
down, it drops the sediment. Sediment then builds up in layers at the
bottom of rivers, lakes, seas, and oceans. These layers are pressed
and stuck together to form sedimentary rocks.

_____

_____

_____

Rewrite this sentence to make it correct.

Igneous rock is rock that was once cooled and hardened but has melted.

Igneous rock is rock that was once melted but has cooled
and hardened.

Harcourt

How Do Rocks Form?

Lesson Concept

There are three types of rocks—igneous, sedimentary, and metamorphic.

Vocabulary

sedimentary rock (C12)   **igneous rock** (C12)

metamorphic rock (C12)   **rock cycle** (C14)

Write the letter of the best answer on the lines.

1. Rocks are grouped by how they __C__.

   A melt   **B** change   **C** form

2. Rocks can be changed by heat and pressure, melting, and the effects of __A__.

   A wind and water   **B** cloud formations   **C** farming

3. After the material from an exploding volcano cools and hardens, __B__ rocks can form.

   A metamorphic   **B** igneous   **C** sedimentary

4. Write about some of the ways you use rocks in the classroom.

   Accept reasonable answers, such as chalk and a chalkboard and

   silicon in computers or calculators.

5. Draw a sedimentary rock.

   Rock should have layers.

Harcourt

Fossil Layers

Materials

5 colors of modeling clay

5 different seashells labeled A through E

5 sheets of wax paper

Activity Procedure

1 Use the chart below.

2 Use clay of one color to make a layer about the size and shape of a hamburger. Put the layer of clay on a sheet of wax paper.

3 Press a shell into the clay to make a print. Remove the shell. **Record** the clay color and the shell letter in your chart.

4 Place a sheet of wax paper over the clay layer.

5 Repeat Steps 2, 3, and 4 until you have made new layers with each color of clay and each shell.

Rock Layer	Clay Color	Shell Letter
1 (bottom layer)		
2		
3		
4		
5 (top layer)		

Harcourt

Name _____

6 Trade your group's clay layers and shells with another group's. Make a second chart. Remove each layer of clay, and **observe** it. Do not change the order of the layers. Match each shell to its print. Fill in the second chart. Check your answers with the group that made the model.

Students may use this space to make a chart like the one on page WB109.

Draw Conclusions

1. How did you know the correct layer for each shell?

The shell shape matched the print in the clay.

_____

2. Pretend the shell prints are fossils and the clay is sedimentary rock. List the shell letters from the oldest to the newest. Do this by using what you know about sedimentary rock layers. Students should indicate that the

shell in the bottom layer is the oldest and that the shell in the top

layer is the youngest.

3. **Scientists at Work** Scientists **use models** to understand how things happen. How did **using a model** help you understand how fossils are left in layers in time order? The model was made the same way fossil

layers form. The oldest part of the model was the bottom layer. The

oldest fossils are in the bottom layers of sedimentary rock. The

newest fossils are in the top layers.

Harcourt

Name _____

Date _____

Process Skills Practice

Use a Model

Think About Using a Model

Shawna decided to make a model of a shell mold to help her understand how fossils are preserved. She mixed up some wet mud and half-filled a plastic margarine tub. She pressed a shell into the mud and covered it with more mud. She let the mud mixture dry in the sun for four days. Then she broke apart the mold, being careful not to disturb the mud below the shell.

1. Why might you use a model to find out about how fossils are preserved?

Accept reasonable answers, which may include making observations

about how impressions are formed in rock by shells or other

animal parts.

2. What problems do you think there would be in recovering fossil prints from hardened mud?

Accept reasonable answers, such as the fact that the imprint

may be broken when the mold is opened.

3. What do you think Shawna saw after she broke open her mold?

Accept reasonable answers, such as the impression of the shell

in the mud.

4. Draw what you think Shawna saw.

Students will likely draw a piece of hardened mud with an

impression of a shell.

Harcourt

Use Prefixes and Suffixes to Determine Word Meaning

What Fossils Are

Underline the prefix or suffix in each term. Then write the root word of each term. Use a dictionary to look up each term, and write its meaning in your own words.

1. fossilize

    root word: fossil

    definition of *fossilize:* to convert into a fossil

2. imprint

    root word: print

    definition of *imprint:* a mark or depression made by pressure

3. prediction

    root word: predict

    definition of *prediction:* an act of predicting

4. preservation

    root word: preserve

    definition of *preservation:* to keep or save from decomposing

What Are Fossils?

Lesson Concept

A fossil is something that has lasted from a living thing that died long ago.

Vocabulary

fossil (C20)

Put a check mark in front of the true statement in each pair.

_____ **1.** Sedimentary rocks usually have more fossils than other rocks because heat and pressure help preserve the fossil.

✓ Sedimentary rocks usually have more fossils than other rocks because what's left of a plant or animal is trapped in the sediments that form the layers of the rock.

_____ **2.** Fossils can show the color of an animal that lived long ago.

✓ Fossils can show the shape of an animal that lived long ago.

✓ **3.** A mold is the shape of a plant or animal left in sediments when the rock formed.

_____ A mold is the imprint of a leaf or another thin object.

✓ **4.** A cast has the exact shape of the animal that made the mold.

_____ A cast always has a small piece of bone in the mold.

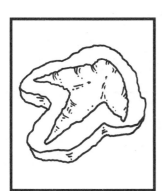

5. Explain how this mold formed.

The animal died. All its soft tissue rotted. The bones were covered with sediment and left an impression in the mud. The sediment hardened and became rock. The bones decayed, leaving their impression in the rock.

Harcourt

Recognize Vocabulary

Fill in the blanks with the correct term from the box. Then find the words and circle them in the word search puzzle.

mineral	**rock**	**crust**	**mantle**
core	**rock cycle**	**fossil**	

1. A solid object that was formed in nature and has never been alive is likely to be a ___mineral___.

2. The surface layer of Earth is called the ___crust___.

3. The ___mantle___ is the middle layer of Earth.

4. At the center of Earth is the hottest layer called the ___core___.

5. A ___rock___ is made of minerals.

6. A ___fossil___ is a thing that has lasted from a living thing that died long ago.

O	F	M	A	N	C	M
R	O	C	K	U	R	A
F	S	T	U	R	A	N
S	S	C	R	U	S	T
M	I	N	E	R	A	L
T	L	T	A	U	L	E
L	E	C	O	R	E	N

Read the sentences. Write the correct letter of the term on the lines.

A metamorphic rock	**B** sedimentary rock	**C** igneous rock

___C___ 7. It is a type of melted rock that has cooled and hardened.

___B___ 8. This rock forms from material that settles into layers.

___A___ 9. Heat and pressure have changed other rocks into this type of rock.

Harcourt

Name _____

Date _____

Write a "Rock" Song

Expressive Writing–Song Lyrics

Write lyrics for a song that describes the rock cycle. Use the idea web below to help you plan your song. Add information about how each type of rock is changed into the others.

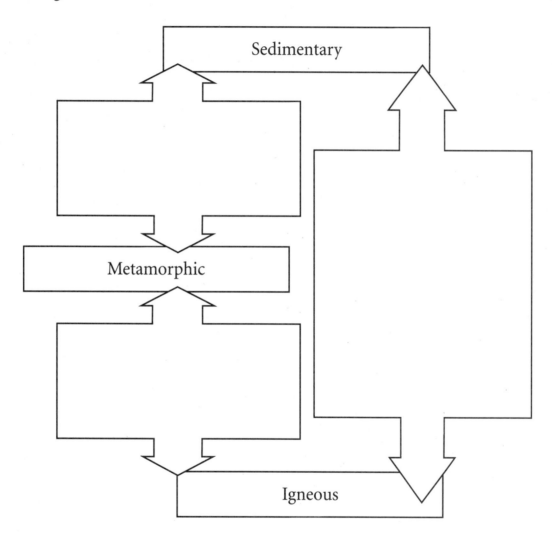

Sedimentary

Metamorphic

Igneous

Harcourt

Chapter 2 • Graphic Organizer for Chapter Concepts

Forces That Shape the Land

LESSON 1
LANDFORMS

Types of Landforms

1. mountains _____
2. valleys _____
3. canyons _____
4. plains _____
5. plateaus _____
6. barrier islands _____

LESSON 2
SLOW LANDFORM CHANGES

Things That Weather Landforms

1. wind _____
2. water _____
3. plants _____

**Things That Erode
Weathered Rock**

4. gravity _____
5. wind _____
6. water _____
7. ice _____

LESSON 3
RAPID LANDFORM CHANGES

Causes of Rapid Changes

1. earthquakes _____
2. volcanoes _____
3. floods _____

Harcourt

Investigate Log

Folds in Earth's Crust

Materials

4 paper towels

plastic cup

water

Activity Procedure

1 Stack the four paper towels on a table. Fold the stack in half.

2 Sprinkle water on the towels. They should be damp but not very wet.

3 Place your hands on the edges of the damp towels.

4 Push the edges slowly toward the center.

Draw Conclusions

1. What happened as you pushed the edges of the towels together?

The towels bunched up and folded in the center.

_____

_____

2. How did the height of the towels change as you pushed them?

The towels were higher in the middle after they were pushed.

_____

_____

Harcourt

Name _____

3. Scientists at Work Scientists **use models** to understand how things happen. How did this model help you understand how mountains form? The towels stood for the Earth's surface. Pushing the towels showed how the surface could be pushed into folds that become mountains.

_____

_____

Investigate Further Some mountains, such as the Rocky Mountains shown on page C33, form when two separate pieces of Earth's crust push together. How would you **make a model** to show this process?

My model: Students could use two identical stacks of damp paper towels. They could also use other objects, such as blocks of soft clay or cloth. As students push these things together, bulges will form where the separate objects or stacks of objects meet.

_____

_____

_____

Harcourt

Name _____

Date _____

Use a Model

Some things, like a flower blooming, take so long to happen, that they are hard to see. Other things, like a frog grabbing a fly with its tongue, happen so quickly that you don't see anything until it's over. You can learn more about something you can't easily see by using a model.

Think About Using a Model

Wong read that folds in Earth's surface can form mountains. The book said that it takes a lot of pressure to fold over the thick surface of Earth. He made a model so he could understand how much pressure. He took one sheet of newspaper and folded it in half. He continued to fold the newspaper in half as many times as he could. With each folding, the number of layers of paper doubled. After seven foldings, there were 128 layers. He observed that as the number of layers increased, he had to use more pressure to fold it.

1. What happened each time Wong folded the newspaper?

   Accept reasonable answers. For example, the number of layers increased, the newspaper became thicker, and he had to use more pressure to fold it.

2. How is Wong's model similar to folds in Earth's surface?

   Accept reasonable answers. Possible answer: The layers of newspaper are like layers of rock on Earth's surface.

3. How did the model help Wong understand the amount of pressure required to fold Earth's crust? Accept reasonable answers. For example, Wong learned that the thicker something is, the more pressure it takes to fold it. Earth's crust is much thicker than the newspaper, so it must take a lot of pressure to fold it.

Harcourt

Use with page C33.

Name _____

Date _____

Use Reference Sources

Earth's Surface

Use reference sources to gather information about the barrier islands in North Carolina called the Outer Banks. Write five fact cards, each telling one fact about the Outer Banks. At the bottom of the fact card, write your source. Cut out your fact cards, and compare them with other students' facts.

Facts About the Outer Banks in North Carolina

Reference Source:
_____

Reference Source:
_____

Reference Source:
_____

Reference Source:
_____

Reference Source:
_____

Harcourt

Use with page C36.

What Are Landforms?

Lesson Concept

Landforms are the shapes, or features, found on Earth's surface.

Vocabulary

mountain (C35)   **valley** (C35)   **plateau** (C35)

landform (C34)   **plain** (C35)   **canyon** (C35)

barrier island (C35)

Write the letter of the best answer on the lines.

1. A _____C_____ is at least 600 meters higher than the land around it.

   A plateau   **B** tall hill   **C** mountain

2. When a river cuts a path through a plateau, a __A__ can form.

   A canyon   **B** barrier island   **C** sand dune

3. Two flat areas on Earth's surface are __B__.

   A valleys and   **B** plains and   **C** caverns and
        canyons   plateaus   mountains

Label each landform. Use the vocabulary list.

4. _mountain_____   **5.** _plateau_____   **6.** _canyon_____

Harcourt

Sand at Work

Materials

sandstone rocks

sand

glass jar with lid

balance

extra masses for balance

Activity Procedure

1 Use the table below.

2 **Measure** the mass of all the rocks. **Record** your results in the table.

3 Fill the jar one-fourth full with sand. **Measure** the mass of the jar with the sand in it. **Record** your results. Add to get the total.

4 Put the rocks into the jar. Put the lid on. Shake the jar for 30 minutes. Then put the jar aside. Shake the jar for 30 minutes every day for one week.

5 After one week, **measure** the mass of the jar and its contents. Then remove the rocks from the jar. **Measure** their mass. **Record** your results. Subtract to find the mass of the jar with the sand inside.

	Mass of Rocks	Mass of Jar and Sand	Total Mass of Rocks, Jar, and Sand
Before			
After			

Harcourt

Name _____

Draw Conclusions

1. What did the sandstone look like before shaking?
   Students will describe the sandstone at the beginning of the
   investigation.

   Did it look different after shaking? How? After one week of shaking,
   the sandstone should show signs of wear, and small pieces
   of sandstone may be present in the sand.

2. Compare the masses before and after the shaking. How did the mass of
   the rocks change? The mass of the rocks decreased.

3. **Scientists at Work** Scientists **interpret data** to understand how things
   work. Use the data from this investigation to tell what happened to the
   sand and the rock.
   Students should conclude that the shaking of the sand against the
   rocks chipped away at the sandstone, just as wind chips away at
   rock by smashing sand against it.

   Investigate further Design an experiment to test this **hypothesis:**
   Larger pieces of rock weather faster.

Harcourt

Name _____

Date _____

Interpreting Data

Data is information given to you or information you gather during activities. When you interpret data, you decide what it means.

Think About Interpreting Data

Andrea gathered data on the wearing away of rocks. She worked with a piece of siltstone and a piece of limestone. Before beginning, she measured each of the rocks and recorded her data. She rubbed a small file back and forth over each rock. The file acted like grains of sand blown by the wind against the rocks. Siltstone is a soft rock, so many pieces fell off as Andrea rubbed the file back and forth. Limestone is a harder rock. Only a few grains fell off.

	Siltstone	**Limestone**
Size at the beginning	6 centimeters	6 centimeters
Size at the end	2 centimeters	5 centimeters
Amount of stone that wore off	4 centimeters	1 centimeter

1. Which stone was larger at the end of the experiment? __limestone__

2. Which stone was smaller at the end of the experiment?
   __siltstone__

3. What do you think the surface of the siltstone would look like after it had been rubbed with the file? Accept reasonable answers. The surface of the siltstone may be smooth and powdery.

4. What is the reason so much more of the siltstone wore off than the limestone? The limestone is harder than the siltstone.

5. How is rubbing a file on the rock like wind wearing away rock?
   Accept reasonable answers. The wind will pick up sand grains and rub the rock like a file; the wind can remove bits of rock like a file.

Harcourt

Name _____

Date _____

Summarize and Paraphrase a Selection

Changes to Land

Read the paragraph. Then make an outline about Sleeping Bear Dunes.

Sleeping Bear Dunes

A dune is formed when wind blows sand into a large mound. One of the world's largest areas of dunes, called Sleeping Bear Dunes, is found in the northwestern part of Michigan's Lower Peninsula. The dunes run along the shore of Lake Michigan and stretch over 11 kilometers (7 mi). The dunes rise about 152 meters (500 ft) above the lake. Beach grass and sand cherry are plants that grow in the dunes. Animals that live in and around the dunes include bobcats, deer, skunks, and porcupines. Sleeping Bear Dunes was named after a Chippewa Indian legend.

I. Dunes

  A. Sleeping Bear Dunes is one of the world's largest areas of dunes.

    1. The dunes run along the shore of Lake Michigan.

    2. The dunes are over 11 kilometers (7 mi) long.

    3. The dunes rise about 152 meters (500 ft) above the lake.

    4. Some plants that grow in the dunes are beach grass and sand cherry.

    5. Kinds of animals found in the dunes are bobcats, deer, skunks, and porcupines.

Harcourt

Concept Review

What Are Slow Landform Changes?

Lesson Concept

Wind, water, gravity, and glaciers slowly shape the land by weathering and eroding rock and soil.

Vocabulary

weathering (C40)　　**erosion** (C42)　　**glacier** (C44)

The following sentences about weathering and erosion are mixed up. Number them in order from 1 to 3.

_3__ **1.** Erosion moves the broken rocks around.

_2__ **2.** Water flows into the holes and cracks in one of the broken rocks. The water freezes. The force of the ice breaks the rock into more pieces.

_1__ **3.** The wind blows hard. It blows against rocks and wears them down. The rocks break apart.

4. Which of these things can break rocks? Circle the letter of your answer.

A wind　　**B** water　　**C** ice　　**D** plants　　**(E)** all of them

5. When Jack was in kindergarten, he saw a fence on the edge of a hill. After a few years, he saw that the fence had moved a few inches down the hill. Creep caused the fence to move. Explain the process of creep.

Creep happens when soil moves down steep hills.

_____

Harcourt

A Model Volcano

Materials

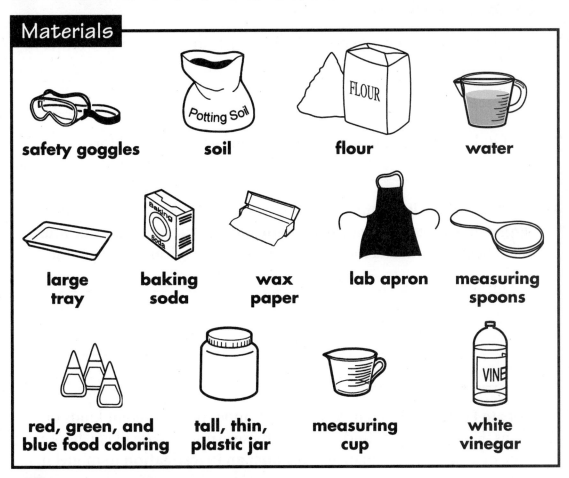

safety goggles   **soil**   **flour**   **water**

large tray   **baking soda**   **wax paper**   **lab apron**   **measuring spoons**

red, green, and blue food coloring   **tall, thin, plastic jar**   **measuring cup**   **white vinegar**

 CAUTION

Activity Procedure

1 Cover the tray with wax paper. Place the jar in the middle of the tray.

2 **CAUTION** **Put on safety goggles and a lab apron.** Mix $\frac{1}{2}$ teaspoon flour and 1 teaspoon baking soda in a measuring cup. Put this mixture into the jar. Add 10 drops of red food coloring.

3 Moisten the soil slightly. Put the soil around the jar. Then mold the soil into the shape of a volcano. The top of the jar must be even with the top of the soil.

4 Slowly pour $\frac{1}{4}$ cup white vinegar into the jar.

5 **Observe** what happens. Remove the jar and throw away the contents. Replace the jar. Then wait 15 minutes for the "lava" to dry.

Harcourt

Name _____

6 Repeat Steps 2, 4, and 5 with the green food coloring and then with the blue food coloring.

Draw Conclusions

1. What happened when you poured the vinegar into the mixture in the jar?
The mixture started to bubble and flowed out of the jar and down
the sides of the volcano model.

2. What did the material that came out of your volcano stand for?
The hot lava that flows from volcanoes.

3. Scientists at Work Scientists **make a model** to understand how things happen in nature that are difficult to **observe** in person. How did your model help you understand the way an erupting volcano changes the
land around it? The liquid flowed out of the model and dried on its
sides. Each time the volcano erupted, another layer was built up.
This is like the liquid rock and ash from a volcano that build layers
on the land around it.

Investigate Further Different kinds of volcanoes have different kinds of eruptions. How could you find out what these eruptions are like? Choose one type of eruption, and **plan and conduct an investigation** to model it.

Type of eruption: _____

Investigation plan: _____

_____

_____

My observations: _____

_____

_____

How this eruption works: _____

_____

_____

Harcourt

Name _____

Date _____

Make a Model

Sometimes you can't observe things because they could hurt you. Other times you can't observe things because you can't get to them. You can make a model to help you understand things in nature that you can't observe in person.

Think About Making a Model

A shield volcano is one kind of volcanic landform. Shield volcanoes have gentle slopes. The lava from shield volcanoes is hot and takes a long time to cool down to become a solid. So when a shield volcano erupts, the lava travels far from the vent. Jonathan knew he couldn't watch an actual shield volcano erupt because it would be too dangerous. He decided to make a model instead.

First he taped a film canister to the center of a piece of cardboard. Next he used clay to shape a mountain around the film canister. He made sure to leave a hole at the top for the lava to come through. When he finished making the mountain, he put in the film canister liquid that erupted like lava.

1. How did Jonathan shape his mountain to make it like a shield volcano?
He made the mountain with gentle slopes, not steep, tall slopes.
_____

_____

2. What did the lava in the model have to do to be like the lava of a shield volcano? It had to flow smoothly down the sides of a mountain.
_____

_____

Harcourt

Use Context to Determine/Confirm Word Meaning

Rapid Changes to the Land

Read the sentences. Look at the underlined words. In the spaces below each sentence, write the clue word or words that might help you know the meaning of the underlined term.

1. The San Andreas <u>fault</u> is a crack in Earth's crust in California.

crack
_____

2. Some earthquakes can cause big sea waves called <u>tsunamis</u>, which can flood coasts.

big sea waves
_____

3. A volcanic <u>eruption</u> can send out hot clouds of ash, rock, and gases.

send out
_____

4. Some volcanic eruptions spill thick, hot <u>lava</u> down the sides of the volcano.

thick, hot
_____

5. If a river can't hold all the rainwater that runs into it, it may overflow its banks and <u>flood</u>.

overflow
_____

Harcourt

What Are Rapid Landform Changes?

Lesson Concept

Earthquakes, volcanoes, and floods can change Earth's surface quickly.

Vocabulary

earthquake (C48)   **volcano** (C49)   **flood** (C50)

Use the vocabulary words above to fill in the blanks.

1. _____Floods_____ can wash away soil and buildings, but leave a new layer of soil on the land.

2. Buildings can be destroyed when an _____earthquake_____ shakes Earth's surface.

3. _____Volcanoes_____ spread lava, ash, or mud in large areas around them.

The following sentences about flooding are mixed up. Number them in the right order from 1 to 5.

__2__ **4.** Rainwater runs into a river.

__1__ **5.** A storm dumps heavy rain on the land.

__5__ **6.** The flood water flows into a farm near the river.

__3__ **7.** The river cannot hold all the water.

__4__ **8.** The river overflows its banks and causes a flood.

Harcourt

Recognize Vocabulary

Match the terms at the right with the definitions on the left.

landform	mountain	valley	canyon
plain	plateau	flood	weathering
erosion	glacier	volcano	earthquake
barrier island			

_____ **1.** the way rocks are broken down into smaller pieces

_____ **2.** movement of weathered rock

_____ **3.** huge sheet of ice that slowly moves downhill

_____ **4.** shaking of Earth's surface by moving of the crust or mantle

_____ **5.** opening in Earth's surface from which lava flows

_____ **6.** large amount of water that covers normally dry land

_____ **7.** shape or feature on Earth's surface

_____ **8.** a place on Earth's surface that is much higher than the land around it

_____ **9.** a lowland area between higher lands, such as mountains

_____ **10.** a deep valley with very steep sides

_____ **11.** a flat area on Earth's surface

_____ **12.** a flat area higher than the land around it

_____ **13.** a thin island near a coast

A mountain

B volcano

C plateau

D barrier island

E weathering

F earthquake

G plain

H erosion

I landform

J glacier

K flood

L valley

M canyon

Harcourt

Use with pages C32–C51.

Write an Editorial

Persuasive Writing–Opinion

Imagine that you are the editor of a science magazine. You have heard that the government will pay for scientists to study one land-changing force. The money should go to the study that helps prevent the worst disasters. Write an editorial telling whether the scientists should use the money to study earthquakes, volcanoes, or floods. Support your opinion with details. Use the organizer below to plan your editorial.

State your opinion.
State reasons. **Reason 1:**
Reason 2:
Reason 3:
Restate your opinion or call for action.

Harcourt

Chapter 3 • Graphic Organizer for Chapter Concepts

Soils

LESSON 1
HOW SOILS FORM

Parts of Soil

1. weathered rock _____

2. humus _____

3. air _____

4. water _____

LESSON 2
HOW SOILS DIFFER

What Makes Soils Different

1. the minerals that make them up _____

2. the size of the mineral particles _____

3. the amount of humus in the soil _____

LESSON 3
CONSERVING SOILS

How Soils Can Be Harmed

1. cutting down trees _____

2. over-farming _____

How Soils Can Be Saved

3. strip cropping _____

4. contour plowing _____

Enrich the Soil

Materials

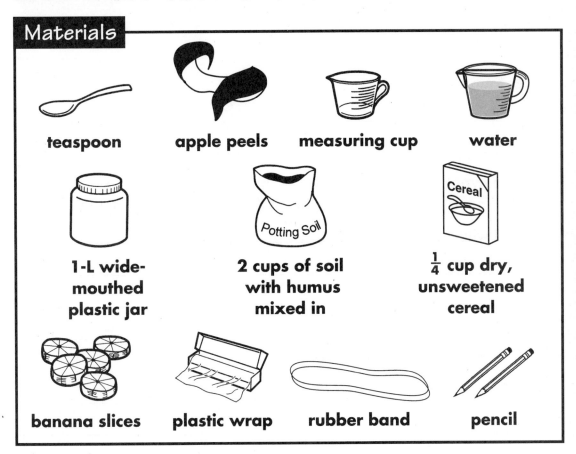

teaspoon

apple peels

measuring cup

water

1-L wide-mouthed plastic jar

2 cups of soil with humus mixed in

$\frac{1}{4}$ cup dry, unsweetened cereal

banana slices

plastic wrap

rubber band

pencil

Activity Procedure

1 Put one cup of soil into the jar. Sprinkle two teaspoons of water on top of the soil.

2 Spread the fruit and cereal on top of the soil. The apple peels and banana slices must touch the sides of the jar.

3 Put another cup of soil on top of the fruit and cereal. You should see pieces of fruit and cereal through the sides of the jar.

4 Cover the jar with plastic wrap. Put a rubber band around the jar to hold the plastic wrap. Use a pencil point to make three small holes in the plastic wrap.

5 Leave the jar in a warm place, but do not put it in direct sunlight. Keep the jar there for four weeks.

6 Look at the jar once each week for four weeks. **Record** what you **observe**.

Harcourt

Name _____

Draw Conclusions

1. What changes did you **observe** in the jar after one week?

The food began to decay.
_____

_____

After four weeks? _____

_____

_____

2. **Form a hypothesis** about what would happen to the soil after eight weeks. To form your hypothesis, finish this sentence: After eight weeks, the soil will. . . . Yes, the material will look different.

_____

_____

Explain. Students should predict that because the food was partly

decayed since it was first left in the jar, it will continue to decay.

_____

_____

3. **Scientists at Work** Scientists use their observations to form hypotheses. How did you use observations to form your hypothesis?

Student answers should express the idea that changes they

saw at first would continue.

_____

_____

Investigate Further **Form a hypothesis** about the effects of compost on plant growth. **Plan an experiment** to test your hypothesis.

Plan: _____

_____

Results: _____

_____

Harcourt

Name _____

Date _____

Hypothesize

Hypothesizing is making a statement about what you think will happen. To make a hypothesis, you use your observations.

Think About Predicting

Plants take in the nutrients they need from the soil in which they grow. Compost is a mixture of rotten plant and animal matter. It is dark-colored and has lots of nutrients in it. Plain soil is light in color and contains few nutrients. Soil becomes darker in color and richer in nutrients as compost is added to it.

Martina's science teacher asked her to grow a cucumber plant. Martina knows cucumber plants need lots of nutrients. Look at the jars of soil below. Help Martina decide which soil to use for her cucumber plant.

1. What do you hypothesize will happen to a cucumber plant in Jar 1?
Explain. Possible answer: The plant will do well in Jar 1 because there are a lot of nutrients in the soil.

2. What do you hypothesize will happen to a cucumber plant in Jar 2?
Explain. Possible answer: The plant will not grow well in Jar 2 because there aren't a lot of nutrients in it. The rocks in the soil will make it difficult for the plant to grow.

3. Which soil should Martina use? Explain. Martina should use the soil in Jar 1 because it has more nutrients from the compost.

Use with page C61.

Harcourt

Name _____

Date _____

Summarize and Paraphrase a Selection

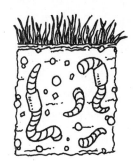

Earthworms

Earthworms make their homes in soil. They need dark, wet places to live. As they make tunnels, worms use the soil for food. When earthworms take particles of soil into their mouths, they don't use all the soil for food. Once the soil is in their bodies, organic material such as bits of plants are used for food. Other materials, such as rock, are passed through each earthworm's body. The waste is then deposited back into the soil.

Earthworms are different sizes and colors. Most earthworms are small, growing to 25 centimeters (10 in.) long. One kind of earthworm from Australia can grow to 3.3 meters (about 11 ft) long! The most common earthworm is reddish-brown. Some earthworms from Britain are green.

1. What are the two main ideas of the selection?

Earthworms live in soil and use it for food. There are different

sizes and colors of earthworms.

2. Write a summary of the selection. Be sure to include information that supports the main ideas of your summary.

Accept reasonable summaries that include information about

the earthworms' home, food, and size and color range.

Harcourt

Use with page C62.

Concept Review

How Do Soils Form?

Lesson Concept

Soil is important to all living things. It takes a long time to form, so we must take care of it.

Vocabulary

soil (C62)   **humus** (C62)   **bedrock** (C63)   **topsoil** (C63)

Write the letter of the best answer on the lines.

1. Soil is a mixture of ___C___ parts.

  A six   **B** three   **C** four

2. Deep soil takes ___C___ to form.

  A 50 years   **B** 500 to 1,000 years   **C** thousands of years

3. Humus is made up of decayed parts of ___B___.

  A rocks   **B** once living things   **C** fossils

4. Soil contains the ___A___ that all living things need for growth.

  A minerals   **B** vegetables   **C** compost

Look at the picture. Label these parts of the soil: topsoil, subsoil, and bedrock.

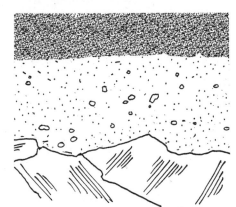

topsoil

_____

subsoil

_____

bedrock

_____

Investigate Log

Types of Soil

Materials

2 soil samples

low-power microscope

toothpick

paper plates

petri dish

paper towel

Activity Procedure

1 Get two soil samples from your teacher.

2 Place a few grains of one sample in the petri dish. Put the dish under the microscope.

3 **Observe** the soil. Move the soil grains around with the toothpick. What do the grains look like? **Record** what you **observe**. Make a drawing of the grains.

My observations: _____

_____

4 Pick up some soil from the petri dish. Rub it between your fingers. How does it feel? **Record** what you **observe**.

My observations: _____

_____

5 Clean the petri dish with the paper towel. Repeat Steps 2 through 4 with the other soil sample.

Harcourt

Name _____

Draw Conclusions

1. What senses did you use to **observe** the soil? sight and touch
_____

2. Describe your observations. Students should describe the size,
shape, color, and feel of the grains.
_____

_____

_____

3. **Scientists at Work** Scientists **observe** to see how things are alike and
how they are different. How were the soil samples alike? How were

they different? All soil is a mixture of weathered rock, humus, water,
and air. Sand grains are larger, lighter, and coarser than potting
soil grains.
_____

_____

_____

_____

Investigate Further Experiment to find another way soils differ. How
much water can different soils hold? Get two different types of soil from
your teacher. Put each type into a separate jar. Now get two cups of water
from your teacher. Pour one of the cups of water into each jar of soil.

Which soil holds more water? The potting soil should retain more water.
_____

_____

How do you know? To find out which soil holds more water, students
can try to pour water from the soil back into the cups and compare the
level of the returned water with the original water level.
_____

_____

Harcourt

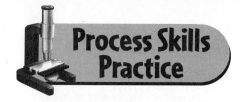

Observe

Sometimes you can tell a lot about something by using only one of
your senses to observe it. Sometimes you can't. You may need to
use more than one sense to observe something.

Think About Observing

Brandon needs to choose soil for a houseplant. He doesn't know whether to
use soil from his backyard or potting soil. The soil from the backyard is light
colored and has a lot of sand in it. The potting soil looks dark and has very
little sand.

   Brandon puts backyard soil in one plant pot and potting soil in another.
Each pot has a hole in the bottom to drain water. He pours a cup of water
into each pot of soil. Most of the water comes out of the pot with the
backyard soil. Very little water comes out of the pot containing potting soil.

Backyard Soil   **Potting Soil**

1. What observations did Brandon make about the samples from looking at
   them? The potting soil is darker than the backyard soil and the
   backyard soil has a lot more sand in it than the potting soil.

2. What observations could he have made with some of his other senses?
   Accept reasonable answers. He could feel the soils' texture. He could
   also smell the soils.

3. If his plant needs a lot of water, which soil should he use? Explain.
   He could use the potting soil because it holds more water than the
   backyard soil. Water will stay in the soil longer, so the plant
   can get to it.

Harcourt

                                    Use with page C67.

Name _____

Date _____

Use Context to Determine/Confirm Word Meaning

Soils and Growing Plants

Use the sentences before and after the underlined terms to write their definitions. Then use a dictionary to look up each term. Complete the chart and compare your definitions.

Some soils are very good for growing plants. Topsoil is a type of soil that is good for growing plants. It is the top layer of the soil and contains the most humus. Humus contains much of what plants need for growth. Humus is the part of the soil made of decayed parts of once-living things. Good topsoils have the right mixture of minerals and humus. Some soils can be changed to make them better for growing plants. Farmers can add fertilizers to poor soils. Fertilizers are materials that are rich in the things plants need for growth.

Your Definition Using Context Clues	Dictionary Definition
topsoil: the top layer of the soil; contains the most humus	**topsoil:** surface soil usually includes the organic layer in which plants have most of their roots
humus: the part of the soil made of decayed parts of once-living things	**humus:** a brown or black material resulting from partial decomposition of plant or animal matter and forming the organic portion of soil
fertilizers: materials that are rich in the things plants need to grow	**fertilizers:** a substance used to make soil more fertile

Harcourt

Use with page C70.

How Do Soils Differ?

Lesson Concept

There are many types of soils. They have different colors and different-sized grains. They also have different mixtures of minerals and humus.

Vocabulary

clay (C69)	loam (C70)

Answer the following questions about soil.

1. Your family fills the backyard sandbox with fresh sand. There is some sand left over. Would it be a good idea to use the sand for planting bean plants? Why or why not? No, sand is too dry and doesn't have a lot of nutrients.

2. Circle each of the elements that help make topsoil good for growing plants.

   A a good mixture of minerals and humus

   B good drainage

   C a high percentage of wet clay

   D plenty of water and air

3. Put a check mark next to the statements that are correct.

   _____ All soils feel the same.   _____✓ Sandy soil feels gritty.

   ___✓___ Some kinds of soil do not hold water.

Underline the best answer.

4. This is rich topsoil with lots of humus, water, and air for plants.

   A clay   **B** loam

5. This soil is made of small grains and feels like powder when it is dry.

   A clay   **B** loam

Harcourt

Saving Soil

Materials

soil

2 wooden blocks

pitcher

2 baking pans

piece of sod

large Styrofoam cup with holes in the bottom

water

Activity Procedure

1. Put soil in both baking pans. Put sod over the soil in one pan.

2. Set one end of each pan on a wooden block. One end of each pan should be lower than the other.

3. **Predict** what will happen when water is dripped into each pan. **Record** your prediction.

   My prediction: _____

   _____

4. **Make a model** of rain over the pan that has just soil. Have one person hold the cup over the upper end of the pan. Have another person pour water from the pitcher into the cup.

5. **Observe** what happens in the pan. **Record** what you see.

   _____

Harcourt

6 Repeat Steps 4 and 5 using the pan that has sod.

My observations of sod: Students should say that there is a lot of soil in the bottom of the pan.

My observations of the soil and sod: Students should say that there is less soil in the pan than in the plain soil pan.

Draw Conclusions

1. What did you **observe** in each pan? **Compare** your observations for the pans. More soil washed away in the soil pan than in the sod pan.

2. What caused the difference? The plants in the sod pan stopped some soil from washing away.

3. Scientists at Work Scientists use their **observations** to **infer** why things happen. Infer how you might keep soil from washing away in the rain. You could plant grass or other plants to keep soil in place.

Investigate Further Plan and conduct an investigation to show how soil can be conserved on the school grounds. For example, grass on the grounds reduces erosion.

Harcourt

Name _____

Date _____

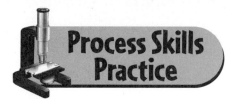

Observe and Infer

When you observe something, you use your senses to study what happens. Inferring is using what you have observed to explain what has happened.

Think About Observing and Inferring

Alicia and Mary wanted to find out how rain erodes bare soil. They dug up two piles of soil about half a meter high. They shaped the piles of soil into mounds. They put a metric ruler into each mound so that only the top 5 centimeters were visible. They put a sheet of newspaper over one of the mounds. Using a watering can, they sprinkled 2 liters of water over each mound. They observed the rulers and noted that the ruler in the uncovered mound showed more centimeter lines than the other.

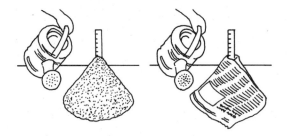

Before Watering

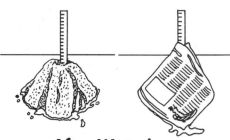

After Watering

1. Describe the mounds before they were watered. _The mounds were the same height. The rulers in them were sticking out the same distance. One mound was bare. The other mound was covered with newspaper._

2. Describe the mounds after they were watered. _The bare mound was shorter than the covered mound. The ruler stuck out more from the top of the bare mound._

3. What inference can you make about bare ground and rain?
If a lot of rain falls on soil that is not covered, the soil may be washed away. If the soil is covered, it might not wash away.

Harcourt

Reading Skills Practice

Use Prefixes and Suffixes to Determine Word Meaning

The -ation and -ing Suffixes

The *-ation* and *-ing* suffixes change an action word (verb) into a word that names the action (noun).

Example

Action word (verb):	conserve
Definition:	to save resources by using them carefully
Suffix:	-ation
New action word (noun):	conservation
Definition:	the act of conserving

Use a dictionary and the sample above to help you complete the information for the terms below.

1. Action word (verb): _restore_

Definition: _to bring something back to its original state_

Suffix: _-ation_

New action word (noun): _restoration_

Definition: _the act of restoring_

2. Action word (verb): _till_

Definition: _to turn over soil_

Suffix: _-ing_

New action word (noun): _tilling_

Definition: _the act of turning over soil_

Harcourt

Name _____

Date _____

How Can We Conserve Soil?

Lesson Concept

Soil that is overused or exposed can erode. Farmers conserve soil by strip cropping, contour plowing, and other methods.

Vocabulary

conservation (C76)   **resource** (C74)

contour plowing (C76)   **strip cropping** (C76)

Write the letter of the best answer on the lines.

1. Soil is important because it is one of Earth's most important _____B_____.
   A products   **B** resources   **C** minerals

2. One way to conserve soil is to plant ___A___ types of crops each year.
   A different   **B** the same   **C** water saving

3. Contour plowing is ___C___.
   A planting thick mats of plants between crops
   B planting low-lying plants that barely cover the ground
   C planting crops around the sides of hills

4. Strip cropping is ___A___.
   A planting strips of thick grass or clover between strips of crops
   B stripping crops when they are ripe
   C putting in dead plant material between plant rows

What can happen to tilled soil during the winter? The bare soil can be lost as wind blows it away or rain washes it away.

_____

Harcourt

Recognize Vocabulary

soil	humus	topsoil
clay	loam	resource
conservation	strip cropping	contour plowing
bedrock		

Read the sentences. Unscramble the scrambled words, and write them on the lines.

1. Lios is the loose material in which plants can grow in the upper layer of Earth.

_____ Soil

2. Shumu is the part of soil made up of decayed parts of once-living things.

_____ Humus

3. Pitools is the top layer of soil.

_____ Topsoil

4. Lyca soil has small grains and small spaces between the grains.

_____ Clay

5. Maol is a rich soil with lots of humus.

_____ Loam

6. A **croesuer** is a material found in nature that living things use.

_____ resource

7. Saving resources by using them carefully is called **scanernotiov**.

_____ conservation

8. Planting strips of grass between crops is called **ripst grocpinp**.

_____ strip cropping

9. Planting crops around a hillside instead of up and down is **toucorn wingolp**.

_____ contour plowing

10. Kcordeb is the solid rock that is underneath the soil.

_____ bedrock

Harcourt

Name _____

Date _____

Write a Letter About Soil

Expressive Writing—Friendly Letter

Write a letter to a friend or family member who lives in
another part of the country. In your letter, tell what you are
learning about soil. Describe the soil where you live. Ask your
friend or family member to write back with a description of the
soil where he or she lives. Use the letter format below to help you
plan your letter.

Heading
Your address:

Today's date:

Greeting
Dear _____ ,

Body of Letter

First Paragraph:

Second Paragraph:

Closing

Your friend,

_____

Harcourt

Chapter 4 • Graphic Organizer for Chapter Concepts

Earth's Resources

WHAT ARE RESOURCES?

Where Resources Are Found

above _____ Earth's surface

Example: air

on _____ Earth's surface

Example: water, forests, soil

under _____ Earth's surface

Example: metals, rocks, minerals

How Resources Are Removed From Earth's Crust

mining in tunnels

strip mining

pumping

DIFFERENT KINDS OF RESOURCES

Renewable Resources

Example: trees or other plants

Two ways these resources are used

paper, food, and furniture

Reusable Resources

Examples: the sun, water, air

Two ways these resources are used

We drink water. We breathe air.

Nonrenewable Resources

Examples: metals, fossil fuels, old growth forests, soil

Two ways these resources are used

to grow food, to make metal objects, to make plastics, as fuel

CONSERVING RESOURCES

Things That Can Be Recycled

aluminum and other metals, glass, paper, plastic

How Resources That Aren't Recycled Can Be Saved

turn off lights, ride your bike, use less water

How You Can Help Reduce Pollution

carpool or ride your bike, turn off lights or find other ways to use less electricity, recycle paper or other materials

Harcourt

Mining Resources

Materials

oatmeal-raisin cookie

dropper

toothpick

paper plate

water

Activity Procedure

1 **Observe** your cookie. How many raisins do you see? _____

2 Fill the dropper with water. Put a few drops of water around each raisin. The cookie should be moist but not wet.

3 Use the toothpick to "mine" all the raisins from the cookie. If the raisins are hard to get out, put a few more drops of water around them. Put the removed raisins on the plate.

4 **Observe** the cookie again. Were there any raisins you didn't see in the cookie the first time? Why didn't you see them?

There probably were raisins that couldn't be seen because they

were inside the cookie.

_____

_____

Harcourt

Draw Conclusions

1. What did you "mine" from the cookie? raisins _____

2. How did the water help you? Water softened the cookie so the raisins could be dug out.

_____

_____

3. How is mining raisins from a cookie like mining materials from the Earth? The raisins had to be dug out of the cookie, just as some resources have to be dug out of Earth's crust.

_____

_____

_____

4. **Scientists at Work** Scientists **observe** things to see how they work. They use their observations to **infer** how similar things work. Use your observations to infer how mining could affect the land around the mine.
When the raisins were mined from the cookie, the cookie was torn up. Afterward it didn't look much like a cookie at all. If land were mined the same way, the land would be torn up like the cookie.

_____

_____

_____

_____

Harcourt

Name _____

Date _____

Observe and Infer

Using your senses helps you observe. You can note what happens in your observations. You then infer by using your observations to form an idea of how things work.

Think About Observing and Inferring

Hydraulic (hy•DRAW•lik) mining is a form of gold mining used in the 1800s. Miners used huge hoses that sprayed water on a cliff. The water washed away chunks of rock. This process ruined the land.

Some students set up an experiment to model hydraulic mining. They buried a number of pebbles in a hill of soil. The pebbles were the models of gold. The students sprayed water on the hill with a garden hose. The water washed away the soil. The pebbles rolled out of the hill.

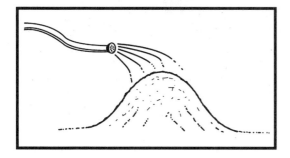 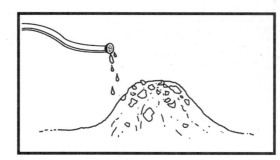

1. What did these students observe before the hill was sprayed and after it was sprayed? Accept reasonable answers. Students may say the soil was all in one mound before it was sprayed. The mound was flattened by the water and a big pile of mud covered the ground. Pebbles could be seen.

2. What was being "mined" in the experiment? pebbles

3. How did the water help remove the pebbles from the hill? The water washed away all of the soil covering the pebbles.

4. What inference can you make about why this is bad for the land? Water can wash away soil and other small particles.

Harcourt

Summarize and Paraphrase a Selection

Oil Is a Resource Important to Your Home

Many resources are important to everyday life in the home. Oil is one important resource that is pumped from Earth's crust.

People use oil for many things. Plastic is made from some of the things found in oil. Plastic is used to make many things, such as food containers, toys, and even the parts of vacuum cleaners.

Gasoline is a fuel that comes from oil. Most cars and trucks use gasoline. Some lawn mowers and weed trimmers use gasoline and oil.

Some homes use oil as fuel for heating. Some power plants burn oil to produce electricity. Electricity is an important power source for most homes. Electricity is used for lights, heat, air conditioning, and appliances.

Oil is a resource that is very important to many people.

Write a summary of the selection. Use your own words.

_____

_____

_____

_____

_____

_____

_____

_____

_____

_____

Harcourt

Name _____

Date _____

What Are Resources?

Lesson Concept

A resource is a material that living things use. We use resources to live and make things we need.

Vocabulary

resource (C88)

1. Circle each resource that is found under Earth's surface.

A oil   **B** air   **C** coal   **D** diamonds

2. Circle each item that is a resource.

A air   **B** animals   **C** water   **D** soil

3. Circle each resource that is found on Earth's surface.

A soil   **B** air   **C** water   **D** oil

4. What are three ways resources are brought up from under Earth's surface?

mining in tunnels
_____

strip mining
_____

pumping
_____

List as many resources as you can that you use during one day.

Accept reasonable answers, such as trees, rocks, metal, air, or
_____   _____   _____

water. Products made from these resources are also acceptable.
_____   _____   _____

_____   _____   _____

_____   _____   _____

_____   _____   _____

Harcourt

Name _____

Date _____

Resource Use

Materials

resource picture cards

product picture cards

Activity Procedure

1 Look closely at all the cards. Sort the cards into two groups—resources and products.

2 **Classify** the products. To do this, match each product with the resource from which it comes.

3 Make a drawing to show how you sorted your cards.

Harcourt

Name _____

Draw Conclusions

1. How did you **classify** the products? Students answers should indicate that they analyzed the products, looking for the materials that helped produce them. Then they matched the products to the appropriate resources.

2. Does a product always look like the resource it was made from? Explain. Not always; resources are changed as they are made into products. Resources such as soil look nothing like the plants that are harvested from them.

3. Scientists at Work Scientists **compare** objects to see how they are alike and how they are different. How did comparing the products to the resources help you **classify** the products? Comparing helped me see which resources were used for which products.

Investigate Further Identify five or more products in your home. **Classify** the products by the resources they came from.

	Products	Resources
1		
2		
3		
4		
5		
6		
7		

Products might include foods grown in soil; furniture made from wood or plastics; clothes made from plants grown in soil; and metal objects, such as pots and pans.

Harcourt

Name _____

Date _____

Compare and Classify

When you compare things, you think about how they are alike and how they are different. Classifying is a way to put objects that are alike into groups.

Think About Comparing and Classifying

The pictures below show three products and three resources from which the products come. Compare the items you see. Identify the products and the resources. Use the chart to list your classifications.

1. Which of these six items can be classified as products?

chair

jacket

gas can

chair

tree

jacket

2. Which of these six items can be classified as resources?

tree

cotton plant

oil

cotton plant

gas can

oil

3. Another way to classify these items is to match each product with the resource from which it comes. Do this by filling in the chart below.

Product	chair	jacket	gas can
Resource from Which It Comes	tree	cotton plant	oil

Harcourt

Use with page C93.

Name _____

Date _____

Identify Cause and Effect

Renewable and Nonrenewable Resources

 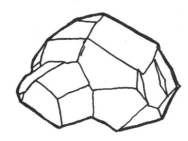

A nonrenewable resource will not last forever. Copper, oil, and iron are examples of nonrenewable resources.

Read the selections below, looking for causes and effects. Underline the cause and circle the effect in each selection.

1. Wood is used for building, and paper comes from trees. When trees are replanted, this resource is renewed for the future.
   cause: trees are replanted; effect: this resource is renewed

2. The sun never stops shining. When the sun shines on Earth, living things use the sun's energy to meet their needs. cause: the sun shines on Earth; effect: living things use the sun's energy to meet their needs

3. People use water for cooking and bathing. Once this water has been dirtied, it must be cleaned before it can be used again. cause: people use water for cooking and bathing; effect: water has been dirtied

4. Some kinds of old growth forests are cut down. It will take hundreds of years for another old growth forest to grow. cause: old growth forests are cut down; effect: it will take hundreds of years for another old growth forest to grow

5. The United States mines a lot of coal. When all the coal has been burned, another fuel will have to be used. cause: all the coal has been burned; effect: another fuel will have to be used

6. People use natural gas to heat homes and cook food. When all the natural gas has been burned, there will be no more for people to use. cause: all the natural gas has been burned; effect: there will be no more for people to use

Harcourt

Use with page C95.

What Are the Different Kinds of Resources?

Lesson Concept

Resources can be renewable, reusable, or nonrenewable.

Vocabulary

renewable resource (C94)   **reusable resource** (C94)

nonrenewable resource (C96)

Make a check mark in front of the statements that are true.

_____ **1.** An old growth forest is a reusable resource.

___✓___ **2.** Soil is a nonrenewable resource.

___✓___ **3.** Water and air are reusable resources.

4. Draw a picture of a reusable resource. Explain why the resource is reusable.

This resource will never run out. It cannot be broken down or will not run out of energy for a long time.

_____

_____

5. Name one nonrenewable resource you care about. Give some ideas for caring for that resource. Accept reasonable answers, as long as the resources named are nonrenewable and the ideas for caring for them are logical.

Harcourt

Recycling

Materials

aluminum cans your family uses in one week	large plastic trash bag	bathroom scale

Activity Procedure

1 Get permission from a parent to participate in this activity. Save all of the aluminum cans your family uses for one week. Rinse them in the sink. Put the cans in the trash bag.

2 Weigh the cans. If your cans are too light to weigh, you can find their weight by multiplying the number of cans you have collected by 1.5 oz. **Record** the weight.

3 Bring your results to class. Use your data to draw a bar on the class graph. The graph will show the weight of each family's cans.

4 Add up all the weights shown on the graph. The sum tells you how much aluminum all the families used in one week.

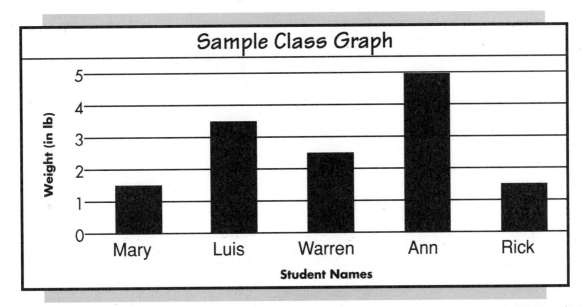

Sample Class Graph

Weight (in lb)

Mary Luis Warren Ann Rick

Student Names

Harcourt

Name _____

Draw Conclusions

1. Suppose that 1 lb of cans takes up 2 ft of space. How much landfill space would your class save by recycling all the cans you saved this week?

This question treats the cans as one-dimensional objects so that students can easily add up the amount of space used. Students should multiply the weight of the cans by 2 ft.

_____

_____

_____

_____

2. What other resources might be saved if your cans were recycled instead of thrown away? Accept reasonable answers. Students may suggest that besides saving the metal used to make the can, the energy used to mine, transport, and refine the ore will also be saved.

_____

_____

_____

3. Scientists at Work There are many ways you could tell someone how much aluminum was used in one week. In this investigation you **used numbers** to describe the weight of aluminum used. How does using numbers help you tell people what you found out?

Using numbers is a more accurate way of describing information than describing in words alone. Also, word descriptions such as "a pile of cans" would mean different things to different people.

_____

_____

_____

Name _____

Date _____

Use Numbers

Using numbers gives you exact amounts of things. You can use numbers to tell others about data you've collected.

Think About Using Numbers

Savannah goes to a recycling center. People drive up and unload their recyclables. Trucks come in filled with newspapers, glass bottles and jars, soda cans, and aluminum food cans. A large sign lists the number and weight of the objects that come in each half-hour. Savannah wants to report back to her class what she sees. She makes a chart. She records the weight of the paper and the number of items recycled while she was there.

Glass	Aluminum	Paper
300 bottles	500 soda cans	1,814 kg
150 jars	250 food cans	

1. List the total number of glass items recorded on the chart. _____450_____

2. List the total number of aluminum cans recorded on the chart. _____750_____

3. A sign at the center says "For every 907 kilograms (2,000 lb) of paper recycled, 17 trees are saved." If the sign is correct, how many trees are saved by recycling 1,814 kilograms of paper? _____34 trees_____

4. How did using numbers help Savannah tell people what she found out?

   She could tell people how many things came into the recycling

   center. She could also tell them how many trees were saved.

   _____

Harcourt

Name _____

Date _____

Use Prefixes and Suffixes to Determine Word Meaning

In the chart below, identify the prefix or suffix in each word. Then identify the root word. Tell how the word with the prefix or suffix is different from the root word. You may use a dictionary to help you.

Conserving Resources

Term	Root Word	Prefix or Suffix	How is the term different from its root word?
reuse	use	re-	*Use* means to make use of; *reuse* means to use again.
healthful	health	-ful	*Health* means well-being; *healthful* means helpful to your health.
unhealthful	health	un- and -ful	*Health* means well-being; *unhealthful* means not good for your well-being.
nonrenewable	renew	non- and -able	*Renew* means to make again; *nonrenewable* means unable to be made again.

Use with page C102.

Harcourt

How Can We Conserve Earth's Resources?

Lesson Concept

We can conserve resources by using fewer resources or by recycling.

Vocabulary

recycle (C100)

Circle the best answer in each sentence.

1. Tuesday is trash pickup day in Jason's neighborhood. Trash is picked up and taken to the **recycling center • landfill** where it is buried in the ground.

2. Jason and his classmates started a **fuel oil • recyclable** collection program in their classroom. They made containers for aluminum cans and glass bottles. They set up some boxes for used paper. The program helped save energy and reduce pollution.

3. Jason decided to find out where the aluminum for their soft drink cans comes from. He learned that aluminum comes from **bauxite • ammonite** ore. The ore is mined. He also learned that aluminum is a nonrenewable resource.

4. Jason's class learned that some resources cannot be recycled, but they can be **conserved • renewed** in a number of ways. Jason decided to turn off lights when he wasn't using them. He decided to walk or ride his bike whenever possible.

5. What are your ideas for recycling and using fewer resources?

   Accept any reasonable answers that may reduce the amount of fuel

   or water used or recycle common household waste.

Harcourt

Vocabulary Review

Recognize Vocabulary

Choose the best term to complete the sentences. Write your
answers on the lines. Use each term only once.

| resources | renewable resources | reusable resources |
| nonrenewable resources | | recycled |

Dear Marsha,

Did you know that living things use materials

called _____resources_____? Some of them

will never be used up. We call

them ____reusable resources____. Air, water, and

the sun are good examples of these. There are also

____renewable resources____. These resources can

be replaced. Replanting trees replaces cut trees.

Some resources, like oil, coal, and metals, are

____nonrenewable resources____. They cannot be

replaced. We need to conserve these so we can

use them longer. Some of these resources can be

_____recycled_____, or used again to

make new products. Aluminum cans can be

melted down and made into new cans.

Your friend,

Lisa

Use with pages C86–C105.

Harcourt

Name _____

Date _____

Write an Essay About Resources

Informative Writing—Compare and Contrast

Write a three-paragraph essay that compares and contrasts the three kinds of resources. For each paragraph's topic, answer these questions:

• How are these resources alike?
• How do they differ from one another?

Use the organizer below to help you plan your writing.

Paragraph Topics	Renewable Resources	Reusable Resources	Nonrenewable Resources
Paragraph 1: What are examples of each kind of resource?			
	How are these resources alike? How do they differ?		
Paragraph 2: How do people use these resources?			
	How are these uses alike? How do they differ?		
Paragraph 3: Are these resources endangered? If so, how?			
	How are these resources alike? How do they differ?		

Harcourt

Use with pages C110–C111.

Chapter 1 • Graphic Organizer for Chapter Concepts

The Water Cycle

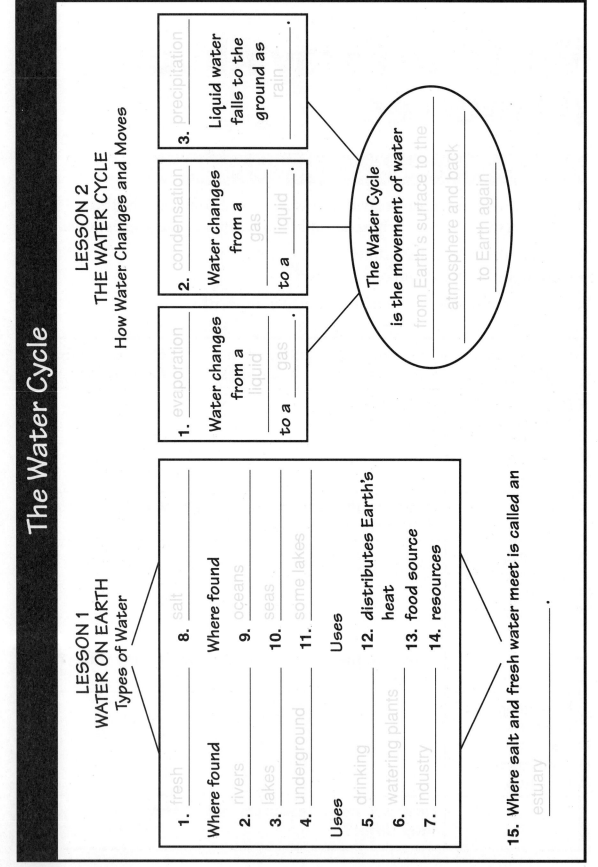

LESSON 2
THE WATER CYCLE
How Water Changes and Moves

3. precipitation
Liquid water falls to the ground as rain .

2. condensation
Water changes from a gas to a liquid .

1. evaporation
Water changes from a liquid to a gas .

The Water Cycle is the movement of water from Earth's surface to the atmosphere and back to Earth again .

LESSON 1
WATER ON EARTH
Types of Water

1. fresh

8. salt

Where found

2. rivers

3. lakes

4. underground

Where found

9. oceans

10. seas

11. some lakes

Uses

5. drinking

6. watering plants

7. industry

Uses

12. distributes Earth's heat

13. food source

14. resources

15. Where salt and fresh water meet is called an estuary .

Harcourt

Land or Water

Materials

plastic inflatable globe

Activity Procedure

1 Work in groups of five. Choose one person to be the recorder. The other four people will toss the ball.

2 Have the four ball tossers stand in a circle. The recorder hands the ball to the first person, who gently tosses the ball to another person in the circle.

3 The catcher should catch the ball with open hands. Check to see if the tip of the catcher's right index finger is on land or water. The recorder should **record** this data.

4 Continue tossing and recording until the ball has been tossed 20 times.

5 Repeat Steps 3 and 4 two more times.

Harcourt

Name _____

Draw Conclusions

1. Total your counts. How many times did the catcher's right index
finger touch water? Touch land? *It is likely that water areas*
will be touched more often.

_____

2. Where did the catcher's fingers land more often? Why do you think so?
Fingers should have landed on water almost three times more

often than on land.

_____

3. Scientists at Work Scientists **use numbers** to **collect data**. Using your
data, estimate how much of Earth's surface is covered by water.
Students should estimate that about $\frac{2}{3}$ of Earth is covered

by water.

_____

Investigate Further You did this investigation 3 times. The more
data you collect, the better your data becomes. How would doing the
investigation 10 times change your data? Try it to find out.
Students should realize that the more times they repeat

the investigation the more reliable their data becomes.

_____

Harcourt

Name _____

Date _____

Collect Data and Use Numbers

When you collect data, you make observations and record them.
Using numbers helps you answer questions.

Think About Collecting Data and Using Numbers

You write to your cousin who lives in another state and tell her what a rainy
year it's been. She writes back and asks what you mean by "a rainy year." You
realize you need to collect data by finding out some rainfall measurements.
You look up the rainfall numbers for one month in the summer and one
month in the winter for this year and last year.

Rainfall in Summer and Winter	
August, this year	Week 1: 5 cm; Week 2: 7 cm; Week 3: 4 cm; Week 4: 2 cm
August, last year	Week 1: 3 cm; Week 2: 5 cm; Week 3: 2 cm; Week 4: 1 cm
February, this year	Week 1: 0 cm; Week 2: 2 cm; Week 3: 1 cm; Week 4: 3 cm
February, last year	Week 1: 0 cm; Week 2: 1 cm; Week 3: 0 cm; Week 4: 2 cm

1. How does collecting data by using numbers help you answer your
   cousin's question? Numbers are a more exact way of providing
   information about how much rain fell.

2. Why is it a good idea to collect rainfall totals for two months, instead
   of just one? by collecting more data you can find more information

3. Total the rainfall counts. How much rain fell in August of each year? How
   much rain fell in February of each year? What is the total amount of rain
   for each year? Was this year really rainy compared to last year?
   Yes, it was rainy compared to last year.

   August, this year: 18 cm   February, this year: 6 cm   Total: 24 cm

   August, last year: 11 cm   February, last year: 3 cm   Total: 14 cm

Harcourt

Name _____

Date _____

Summarize and Paraphrase a Selection

Read the selection about the Ogallala aquifer. Then fill in the chart with the main idea and supporting details in your own words.

The Ogallala Aquifer

An aquifer is a large area of groundwater. An aquifer has enough water to supply many wells. The Ogallala aquifer lies beneath part of northwestern Texas and a small part of eastern New Mexico. For over 100 years, the Ogallala has provided water to cities, towns, ranches, and farms. The Ogallala supplies 170,000 wells. Every year, more and more water is taken from the Ogallala. Currently, about 6 billion cubic meters of water is used a year. Unfortunately, nature cannot replace all of the water that is used. Water experts are encouraging people to conserve water. They hope this will help the aquifer last for many more years.

Main Idea	Supporting Details
The Ogallala aquifer is a large area of groundwater in north-western Texas and part of eastern New Mexico.	It has been around over 100 years.
	It provides water to cities, towns, ranches, and farms.
	It supplies 170,000 wells.
	People use 6 billion cubic meters of water from the aquifer.
	Not all of the water used is replaced.
	Water experts hope people will conserve the water so it lasts many more years.

Harcourt

Concept Review

Where Is Water Found on Earth?

Lesson Concept

More than two-thirds of Earth's surface is covered with water.
Most water on Earth is found in the oceans.

Vocabulary

groundwater (D8)   **estuary** (D12)

**As you read the summary, fill in the blank with one of the
vocabulary terms from above.**

Without water there could be no life on Earth. Plants, animals, and people
need water to live. Water is important to Earth's environment. Water helps
cause winds and storms, and it changes the shape of Earth's surface. Only a
small amount of Earth's water is fresh water. The rest is salt water found in
the oceans. Water that is under Earth's surface is called

_____groundwater_____. There are places called _____estuaries_____

where fresh water and salt water meet.

Answer each question with one or more complete sentences.

1. What are some ways you could conserve, or save, water each day?

Answers could include taking short showers, turning off the water

while brushing teeth, or planting plants that don't need a lot of water.

Accept all reasonable answers.

2. Describe how groundwater gets under Earth's surface.

Groundwater begins as rain that soaks into the soil. It moves

down through the soil and broken rocks until it reaches solid rock.

Harcourt

Name _____

Date _____

Evaporation

Materials

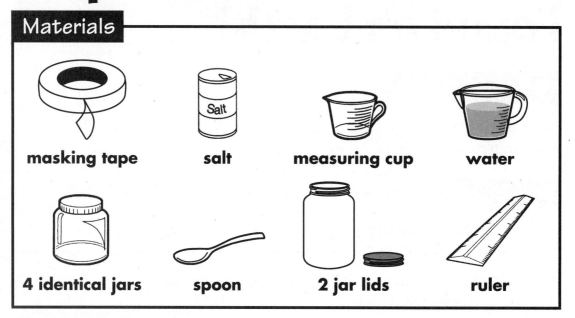

masking tape   salt   measuring cup   water

4 identical jars   spoon   2 jar lids   ruler

Activity Procedure

1. Put a strip of masking tape down the side of each jar.

2. Using the measuring cup, pour $\frac{1}{2}$ cup water into each jar. Stir a spoonful of salt into 2 of the jars. Mark these jars with an *S*. Mark the other 2 jars with an *F*.

3. Make a mark on the tape on each jar to show how high the water is. Then put the lids on one *S* jar and one *F* jar.

4. **Predict** from which jar the water will evaporate first. **Record** your prediction.

5. Place the jars in a sunny place.

6. **Observe** the jars every day for a week. Each day, mark how high the water in each jar is.

Harcourt

Name _____

Investigate Log

Draw Conclusions

1. Did all the water evaporate from any of the jars? If so, which one?

Answers will vary but the jar with fresh water will evaporate first.

2. Compare your prediction with your results. How did you make your prediction? Was your prediction correct? Accept reasonable responses. Students should have based their predictions on personal observations of the world around them.

3. Scientists at Work To find the answers to some questions, scientists test things that will change. These things are called *variables*. Then they add something to the experiment that they know won't change. This is called a *control*. What were the controls in this investigation?

The jars with the lids were the controls. With the lids on, the water inside couldn't evaporate.

Investigate Further Infer what would happen if you repeated the activity but used different amounts of salt. How would the results change? Try the activity to see if your inference was correct. Don't forget to use controls.

The saltier the water, the slower its evaporation rate.

Harcourt

Control Variables

Controlling variables is a way to make sure that experiments are fair tests. But before you can control variables, you have to know what the variables in your experiment are.

Think About Controlling Variables

Jessie wanted to do another investigation of water evaporation. She thought about the variables in her experiment. She came up with the following list.

Variable 1. the size of the water sample

Variable 2. the kind of water used

Variable 3. the shape of the container

Variable 4. the amount of time each sample was on the windowsill

Jessie wanted to control all but one variable, the shape of the container. She put one cup of water into a tall, thin drinking glass. Then she poured one cup of water into a cereal bowl. The water for both containers came from the same water bottle. Jessie placed the glass and the bowl on a sunny windowsill. She recorded her observations. Jessie noticed the water in the bowl evaporated more quickly than the water in the glass.

1. Why do you think the water evaporated more quickly from the bowl?

The shape of the container exposed more of the water to the air
and, therefore, had something to do with the evaporation.

2. What would have happened if Jessie had controlled all but Variable 1?

The smaller sample would have evaporated first.

3. What would have happened if Jessie had controlled all but Variable 2?

It depends on the kind of water used. The investigation has already
shown that salt water, for example, will take longer to evaporate.

Harcourt

Name _____

Date _____

Use Context to Determine/Confirm Word Meaning

How Water Changes

Look at the sentences below. Circle word clues or phrases that help define the underlined term. Write what you think the term means based on the clues. Then use the glossary in your science book or a dictionary to look up each term to check your answers.

1. The form that water takes depends on the amount of heat, or <u>thermal energy</u>, in it.

   thermal energy: heat
   _____

   _____

2. Water is in the air around you in the form of a gas you can't see called <u>water vapor</u>.

   water vapor: invisible gas
   _____

   _____

3. Heat must be added to a liquid to make it <u>evaporate</u>. Evaporation changes liquid water into water vapor.

   evaporate: to change from a liquid to a gas
   _____

   _____

4. During <u>condensation</u>, taking heat away from a gas, or cooling it, changes the gas into liquid.

   condensation: gas changing to liquid after heat is taken away
   _____

   _____

Harcourt

Use with page D18.

Concept Review

What Is the Water Cycle?

Lesson Concept

The water cycle is the movement of water from Earth's surface into the air and back to the surface again.

Vocabulary

evaporation (D17)	**condensation** (D17)
precipitation (D18)	**water cycle** (D18)

Underline the best answer.

1. The form water takes depends upon the amount of ____ in it.

    A condensation **B** water vapor   **C** thermal energy   **D** gas

2. You pour a glass of soft drink and put some ice cubes in it. You leave the glass outside in the sun. The sun changes the ice into ____.

    A liquid water   **B** condensation **C** water vapor   **D** evaporation

3. Earth uses the same water over and over again. The water you use today is ____ years old.

    A 5,000   **B** 500   **C** 10,000   **D** billions of

Fill in the answers.

4. What three forms can water take? _____liquid, as water; solid, as ice;_____

_____gas, as water vapor_____

5. _____Evaporation_____ is the changing of a liquid into gas.

6. _____Condensation_____ is the changing of a gas into a liquid.

7. _____Precipitation_____ is water that falls to Earth as rain, snow, sleet, or hail.

8. _____Water Cycle_____ is the movement of water into the air and back again.

Harcourt

Name _____

Date _____

Recognize Vocabulary

In the space provided, write the letter of the term in Column B that best fits the definition in Column A. Use each term only once.

Column A

_F___ **1.** Rain that soaks into soil and rocks

_E___ **2.** Where fresh water mixes with salt water

_A___ **3.** Changing of a liquid to a gas

_C___ **4.** Water that falls from the sky to Earth

_B___ **5.** Changing of a gas to a liquid

_D___ **6.** Movement of water from Earth's surface into air and back to Earth's surface again

Column B

A evaporation

B condensation

C precipitation

D water cycle

E estuary

F groundwater

Choose two of the vocabulary words from Column B. Then, using your own words, write a sentence that uses each word correctly.

_____

_____

_____

_____

_____

_____

Harcourt

Name _____

Date _____

Tell a Story from the Water Cycle

Narrative Writing—First-person Story

Imagine that you are a raindrop or a snowflake. Tell the story of your life. Use what you know about the water cycle to make your story accurate and interesting. The story map below will help you plan your narrative.

Character (raindrop or snowflake):	Setting (climate region):
Where does your story begin?	
What happens to make you a raindrop or a snowflake?	
What do you see on your journey?	
Where does your story end?	

Harcourt

Use with pages D24–D25.

Chapter 2 • Graphic Organizer for Chapter Concepts

Observing Weather

LESSON 1
WEATHER

Properties of Air

1. takes up space _____

2. has weight; presses _____
   on things _____

3. has layers _____

LESSON 2
MEASURING WEATHER

What Is Measured and How It Is Measured

1. Temperature _____
   is measured with a
   thermometer _____

2. Precipitation _____
   is measured with a rain gauge or snow board.

3. Wind _____
   is measured with a
   wind vane _____
   and an
   anemometer _____

LESSON 3
FORECASTING WEATHER

How Data Is Gathered

1. weather station _____

2. satellites _____

3. planes _____

4. balloons _____

Things Shown on a Weather Map

1. temperature _____

2. precipitation _____

3. wind speed and direction _____

4. fronts _____

Harcourt

Properties of Air

Materials

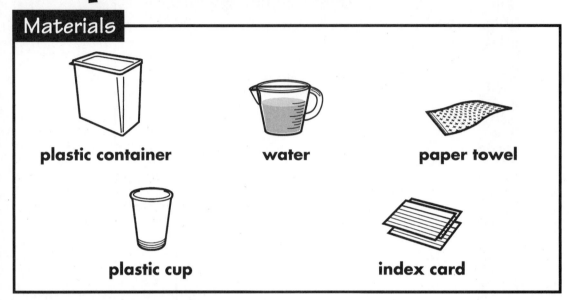

plastic container

water

paper towel

plastic cup

index card

Activity Procedure

Part A

1 Half-fill the plastic container with water.

2 Crumple the paper towel. Push it to the bottom of the plastic cup.

3 Turn the cup upside down. Push the cup to the bottom of the plastic container. Do not tilt the cup as you are pushing it downward. Then pull the cup straight up and out of the water. **Observe** the paper towel. **Record** your observations.

Part B

4 Remove the paper towel from the cup. Half-fill the cup with water. Put the index card over the cup opening.

5 Hold the cup over the plastic container. Use your right hand to hold the cup and your left hand to hold the index card in place. Quickly turn the cup over. Take your left hand off the index card. **Record** your observations.

Harcourt

Name _____

Draw Conclusions

1. What did you **observe** in Part A? The water did not enter the cup; the paper towel stayed dry.

2. What did you **observe** in Part B? The index card stayed in place when the hand was removed from the index card.

3. **Scientists at Work** Scientists **observe** things that happen all around them. They use their observations to **infer** why those things happen. Use your observations to infer one property of air for each part of this investigation. In Part A the water could not enter the cup because air was already inside; in Part B something held the index card in place. There was nothing outside but air. So air must have been pressing on the index card. Possible inferences: air takes up space, air exerts pressure.

Investigate Further Suppose you repeat Part B with a cup that is almost filled with water. **Predict** what will happen. Then try it. Results will be the same, since air pressure will still hold the index card in place.

Harcourt

Name _____

Date _____

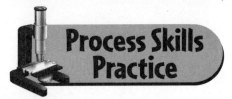

Observe and Infer

When you observe, you use your senses to examine things. Then you can record what you observe.

Think About Observing and Inferring

Suppose you do the following investigation. You put a funnel in the neck of a glass bottle. You fill the space around the funnel with modeling clay, making sure the clay is packed tightly. You pour water slowly into the funnel. You observe that no water goes into the bottle. Then you repeat the experiment. This time you pour water into the funnel, almost to the top. Then you carefully use a nail to poke a hole through the clay to the inside of the bottle. Now water flows through the funnel into the bottle.

1. In the first experiment, you observed that no water flowed through the funnel. Why do you think this is so? Water could not enter the bottle because air was already inside.

2. What do you think this shows about air? Even though air cannot be seen, it is present.

3. In the second experiment, you observed that no water flowed into the bottle until you poked a hole in the clay. Why do you think the water could flow into the bottle? Answers should show that the student understands a hole in the clay allowed the air to escape, so that the water could take its place.

4. What inference could you make about the purpose of the clay? Answer should show that students understand the clay formed a seal to keep the air in the bottle.

Harcourt

Use with page D29.

Use Context to Determine/Confirm Word Meaning

Kinds of Storms

Weather changes all the time. Weather is what is happening in the atmosphere at a certain place. Many kinds of storms happen in different weather systems. <u>Blizzards</u> are large snowstorms. They have low temperatures and strong winds. Often there is so much snow blowing that it is hard to see. <u>Hurricanes</u> also have strong winds. But hurricanes form over warm ocean waters and usually travel over open ocean or along coastlines. A <u>tornado</u> is a violent windstorm with winds so strong that they can destroy buildings and lift cars right off the ground! <u>Ice storms</u> are very dangerous. During an ice storm, freezing rain falls to Earth and freezes immediately. When the ice builds up, it can make road surfaces slick and travel dangerous.

1. What are some word clues that help you know what a <u>blizzard</u> is?

snowstorm, low temperatures, strong winds, blowing snow

2. What are some word clues that help you know what a <u>hurricane</u> is?

strong winds, form over warm ocean waters, travel along coastlines

3. What are some word clues that help you know what a <u>tornado</u> is?

violent windstorm, strong winds destroy buildings, lift cars

4. What are some word clues that help you know what an <u>ice storm</u> is?

freezing rain, ice builds up, slick road surfaces

Harcourt

What Is Weather?

Lesson Concept

Weather is what is happening in the atmosphere at a certain place.

Vocabulary

atmosphere (D30)   **weather** (D32)

Write your answers to the questions.

1. What are the three properties of air? Air takes up space, has weight, and exerts pressure.

2. What do meteorologists do? Meteorologists study weather and the atmosphere, measure and record changes in the air, and predict weather.

3. How does the atmosphere help Earth? Possible answers: it acts like a blanket; it holds in the heat; it keeps us warm; without it, the energy that keeps Earth warm would escape into space.

Underline the best answer.

4. What absorbs harmful rays from the sun?
   A atmosphere   **B** troposphere   **C** ozone   **D** air particles

5. Weather takes place in ____.
   A the air layer farthest away from Earth
   B the air layer closest to Earth

Harcourt

Measuring Temperature

Materials

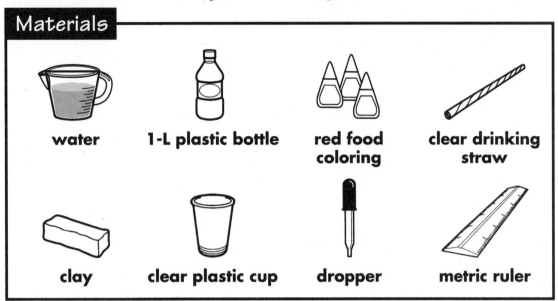

water

1-L plastic bottle

red food coloring

clear drinking straw

clay

clear plastic cup

dropper

metric ruler

Activity Procedure

1 Put water in the bottle until it is almost full. Add 10 drops of food coloring.

2 Put the straw in the bottle. Three-fourths of the straw should stick out of the bottle. Seal the opening around the straw with clay.

3 Half-fill the cup with water. Add three drops of food coloring.

4 Use the dropper to put water from the cup into the straw. Add water until you can see the water in the straw above the clay stopper.

5 Make a mark at the water level in the straw. You have made a thermometer. The higher the level of liquid in the straw, the higher the temperature.

6 Take the thermometer to five different places at school. Leave it at each place for 15 minutes. Use a ruler to **measure** the water level in the straw from the mark to the top of the water level. Do not squeeze the bottle while you measure. **Record** the measurement and the location.

Harcourt

Draw Conclusions

1. What happened to the water levels in the straw in the different locations?

The water levels rose and fell in the different locations.

_____

_____

_____

2. What information could you learn by using your thermometer?

You can tell if one place is warmer or cooler than another based on

the level of water.

_____

_____

What information is impossible to learn by using your thermometer?

You cannot get exact temperatures.

_____

_____

3. **Scientists at Work** Scientists sometimes **use numbers** to put things in order. Look at the numbers you recorded. Use the numbers to order the

locations from warmest to coolest. Answers will vary depending

on where students took measurements. The warmer the area, the

higher up the straw the liquid will have moved.

_____

_____

Harcourt

Use Numbers and Compare

You can use numbers to put things in order and to compare one
set of things to another.

Think About Using Numbers and Comparing

At science camp in August, Jane and two other campers made thermometers
like the one you made in the investigation. On a hot day, they took their
thermometers to three different places outside. After fifteen minutes, they
checked their thermometers. They had a surprise! The water had risen to the
same level on each thermometer. All the temperatures were the same. Then
they took their thermometers to three different places inside the dining hall.
This time the water was at a different level on each thermometer.

1. How did the campers know the temperatures were the same in the first

three locations? because the water had risen to the same point on
the straw in each thermometer

2. Why do you think the water level was the same on each thermometer at

the first location? because the temperature was the same in each of
the three locations

3. What did the water levels tell them at the second location, inside the

dining hall? The temperatures were different at each of the three
locations in the dining hall.

4. Imagine that you were at science camp. Where would you choose to leave

your thermometer? Answers will depend on individual choice.
Accept all reasonable answers.

5. Predict the temperature at the location you chose. Will it be warm or

cool? Explain. Answers will depend on the choice made in Question 4.
Accept any reasonable answers.

Harcourt

Summarize and Paraphrase a Selection

Read the selection below. Write the main idea of the paragraph on the lines below. Then use your own words to write captions for each picture to help summarize the selection.

Wind

Wind is the movement of air. Wind can be helpful. It can cool you on a hot day or it can help you fly a kite. Wind can clean up pollution from the air. Some days it may feel as if there is no wind! Sometimes having not enough wind can be frustrating. A sailboat doesn't get very far when there isn't much wind. It may make things difficult when winds are strong, but people still manage. Often, just walking on a windy day can be difficult. It may be hard to keep your hat and coat on! A strong wind in a rainstorm can turn an umbrella inside out. Unfortunately, winds also can be very damaging. During strong storms such as tornadoes, wind can knock trees over and even destroy buildings.

Main Idea: Wind is air movement. _____

_____

Possible answers: 1. Wind can be helpful when you are flying a kite.
2. Using a sailboat is difficult if there is little or no wind. 3. When winds
are stronger, just walking can be difficult. 4. During a tornado, winds
can be damaging and destroy buildings.

Harcourt

Concept Review

How Are Weather Conditions Measured?

Lesson Concept

Weather conditions are measured with tools such as thermometers, rain gauges, and anemometers.

Vocabulary

temperature (D36)   **front** (D37)

anemometer (D40)   **wind** (D40)

Read the summary. Then answer the questions that follow.

Temperature is a measure of how warm or cold something is. Air temperature is always changing. A large body of air with the same temperature and moisture is called an air mass. Precipitation is any kind of water that falls from the sky. Meteorologists use rain gauges and snow boards to measure precipitation. Wind is the movement of air. A tool called an anemometer is used to measure wind speed.

Underline the best answer.

1. Thermometers can be used to measure ____.

   A temperature   **B** rainfall   **C** air pressure   **D** wind speed

2. A large body of air with the same temperature and moisture is called ____.

   A a front   **B** a cloud   **C** air pressure   **D** an air mass

3. An anemometer measures ____.

   A air pressure   **B** precipitation   **C** wind speed   **D** flood possibilities

4. Rain gauges and snow boards are used to measure ____.

   A air pressure   **B** precipitation   **C** moisture   **D** rainfall

Harcourt

Reading Weather Maps

Materials

weather map

Activity Procedure

1 Study the weather map and the key to the symbols that it uses.

2 Use the map to answer the questions.

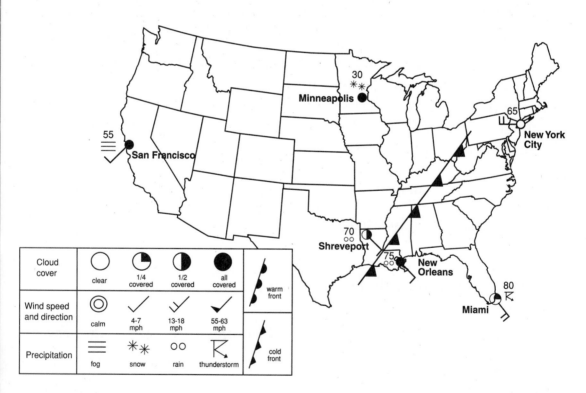

Harcourt

Name _____

Draw Conclusions

1. Where is there a thunderstorm? Miami, Florida _____

2. Find the cold front. What can you tell about the weather along the
   cold front? It is cool, rainy, and cloudy. _____

   _____

   _____

3. **Scientists at Work** Scientists **interpret data** on weather maps to learn
   about the weather in different places. Interpret data on this map to
   describe the weather in Minneapolis, Minnesota. The weather in
   Minneapolis is cloudy and 30° F, and it is snowing.

   _____

   _____

Investigate Further The weather in the United States generally moves from
west to east. Imagine that you are in New York City. Use the data on the map
to **predict** what your weather may be like about one week from now.
Students should indicate that the weather currently in Minneapolis likely
will be affecting New York City in a week's time. Thus the weather there
will be cold and snowy.

_____

_____

_____

Harcourt

Name _____

Date _____

Interpret Data

Data is information given to you or information that you gather during activities. When you interpret data, you decide what it means.

Think About Interpreting Data

The table that follows shows a daily weather report for five days. Interpret the data, and answer the questions that follow.

Daily Weather Report			
Day	**Temperature**	**Precipitation**	**Precipitation Symbol**
Monday	29°C (84° F)	Rain	o o
Tuesday	26°C (79° F)	Rain	o o
Wednesday	24°C (75° F)	Sunny	
Thursday	26°C (79° F)	Fog	=
Friday	29°C (84° F)	Thunderstorm	R

1. What was the coolest day? _Wednesday_

2. On which days did it rain? _Monday, Tuesday, and Friday_

3. Compare the weather on Monday and on Wednesday. Which day would have been better for outdoor exercise? Explain your answer.

Monday was rainy and hot. Wednesday was sunny and cooler.

Wednesday would have been better for outdoor exercise.

4. Which day would have been the worst day to be outside? Explain.

Friday, because there was a thunderstorm

5. Use the symbols you learned in the investigation to fill in the last column of the table.

Harcourt

Name _____

Date _____

Use Graphic Sources for Information

Use the information from the map to answer the questions below.

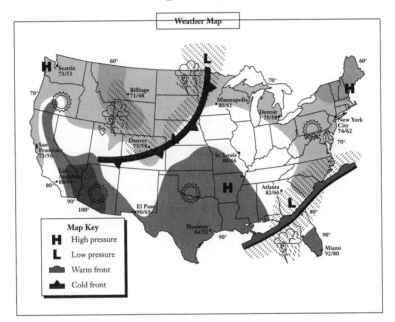

1. How high might the temperature reach in San Francisco?

73 degrees

2. What kind of pressure system is in Seattle?

high pressure

3. Name two things that describe the weather south of Atlanta.

low pressure, rain, warm front

4. What is the expected low temperature in Minneapolis?

61 degrees

5. What city had a cold front and low-pressure system pass through it?

Denver

6. Which city is showing the highest temperature?

Houston

Harcourt

Concept Review

What Is a Weather Map?

Lesson Concept

There are a number of ways to gather weather data. A weather map uses symbols to show weather conditions over large areas.

Vocabulary

weather map (D46)

Write your answers to the following questions.

1. List four kinds of weather data that a weather map shows.

Answers may include precipitation, temperature, warm fronts, cold

fronts, high air pressure, and low air pressure.

2. List four ways that information about weather is gathered.

weather planes, weather balloons, satellites, and ground stations

Underline the best answer.

3. Weather balloons gather data on temperature, precipitation, and ____.

A clouds and storms   **C** wind

B ocean temperatures   **D** storms

4. Weather data collected by the National Weather Service goes into computers that organize the information into ____.

A maps   **C** rain chances

B cloud readings   **D** storm warnings

Harcourt

Name _____

Date _____

Recognize Vocabulary

Read each sentence. Find the missing term in the box below.
Write the correct term on the line.

weather map	**anemometer**	**wind**	**temperature**
precipitation	**atmosphere**	**front**	**weather**

1. A map that shows weather data for a large area is called a

_____weather map_____.

2. The air that surrounds Earth is the ____atmosphere____.

3. An ____anemometer____ is a tool that measures wind speed.

4. An occurrence that happens in the atmosphere at a certain place is called

_____weather_____.

5. Any kind of water that falls to Earth is ____precipitation____.

6. ____Temperature____ is a measure of how warm or cold

something is.

7. The movement of air is ____wind____.

8. A place where two air masses of different temperatures meet is a

_____front_____.

Harcourt

Explain a Thunderstorm

Informative Writing–Explanation

Imagine that you are helping out at a summer camp for younger children. The children may be frightened by thunderstorms. Write a short speech that you could give to younger children, explaining how a thunderstorm happens. Use colorful words to catch the children's imagination. Complete the outline below to help you plan your speech.

Step 1: What happens when a cold front hits warm air?
Step 2: What makes a thunderhead form?
Step 3: What happens when air moves rapidly up and down?
Step 4: Which comes first—thunder or lightning?
Step 5: What happens when the air cools?

Harcourt

Chapter 3 • Graphic Organizer for Chapter Concepts

Earth and Its Place in the Solar System

LESSON 1
WHAT IS THE SOLAR SYSTEM?

Inner Planets

1. Mercury _____

2. Venus _____

3. Earth _____

4. Mars _____

Outer Planets

5. Jupiter _____

6. Saturn _____

7. Uranus _____

8. Neptune _____

9. Pluto _____

Other Objects in the Solar System

10. asteroids _____

11. comets _____

LESSON 2
WHAT CAUSES EARTH'S SEASONS?

Movement of Earth in Space

1. revolution _____

2. rotation _____

Seasons

3. caused by Earth's revolution _____
around the sun

Day and night

4. caused by Earth's rotation _____
on its axis

LESSON 3
HOW DO THE MOON AND EARTH INTERACT?

Phases of the Moon

1. new moon _____

2. first quarter _____

3. full moon _____

4. third quarter _____

Eclipses

5. Lunar eclipses are caused by Earth _____
casting a shadow on the moon

6. Solar eclipses are caused by the moon _____
casting a shadow on Earth

Name _____

Date _____

The Planets

Materials

pencil · planet picture cards (optional) · paper

Planet Data

Planet	Distance from Sun (in millions of kilometers)	Distance Across (in kilometers)	Length of Year (y = Earth year) (d = Earth day)
Earth	150	12,750	365 d
Jupiter	778	143,000	12 y
Mars	228	6,800	2 y
Mercury	58	4,900	88 d
Neptune	4,505	49,000	165 y
Pluto	5,890	2,300	248 y
Saturn	1,427	120,000	29 y
Uranus	2,869	51,000	84 y
Venus	108	12,000	225 d

Activity Procedure

1. Record your answers in the Ordering Planet Data Chart on the next page.

2. **Use numbers** from the data table to find each planet's distance from the sun. **Record** in your chart the names of the planets, beginning with the one closest to the sun.

3. **Use numbers** from the data table to find the distance across each planet. The planet with the shortest distance across is the smallest planet. Use numbers to **order** the planets by size. **Record** the names of the planets in order, beginning with the smallest planet.

Harcourt

Name _____

Ordering Planet Data		
Closest to the Sun to Farthest from the Sun	**Smallest to Largest**	**Shortest Year to Longest Year**
Mercury	Pluto	Mercury
Venus	Mercury	Venus
Earth	Mars	Earth
Mars	Venus	Mars
Jupiter	Earth	Jupiter
Saturn	Neptune	Saturn
Uranus	Uranus	Uranus
Neptune	Saturn	Neptune
Pluto	Jupiter	Pluto

Draw Conclusions

1. Which planet is closest to the sun? Farthest away? __Mercury; Pluto__

_____

2. Which is the largest planet? The smallest? __Jupiter; Pluto__

3. **Scientists at Work** Scientists sometimes **use numbers** to put things in **order**. Scientists have studied the same data you used in this

investigation. __Using numbers allows students to determine each__

__planet's distance from the sun and thus place them in order from__

__the sun.__

Investigate Further Plan and conduct an experiment that **makes a model** to show one set of your planet data. You may wish to use the planet picture cards in your model.

Harcourt

Use Numbers

You can use numbers to order things and put them into groups.

Think About Using Numbers

Suppose you want to group the planets in a number of different ways.
Look at the table that follows.

Planet	Distance Across (in kilometers)
Earth	12,750
Jupiter	143,000
Mars	6,800
Mercury	4,900
Neptune	49,000
Pluto	2,300
Saturn	120,000
Uranus	51,000
Venus	12,000

1. Study the distance across each planet. Group the four largest planets
together. Jupiter, Saturn, Uranus, and Neptune

_____

2. Now study the distances across again, and group the five smallest planets
together. Earth, Mars, Mercury, Venus, and Pluto

_____

Harcourt

Name _____

Date _____

Use Prefixes and Suffixes to Determine Word Meaning

Read the sentences below. Then determine which word in each sentence contains a prefix or a suffix. Write the word, the root word, and a definition below the sentence.

1. Jupiter is the largest planet in our solar system.

Word: largest _____

Root word: large _____

Definition of word: biggest _____

2. Mercury is the hottest planet in our solar system.

Word: hottest _____

Root word: hot _____

Definition of word: most hot _____

3. Mars is colder than Earth.

Word: colder _____

Root word: cold _____

Definition of word: more cold _____

Harcourt

What Is the Solar System?

Lesson Concept

The solar system has nine planets that orbit the sun. Earth is one of those planets. Asteroids and comets are also parts of the solar system.

Vocabulary

solar system (D58)   **orbit** (D58)   **planet** (D58)

asteroid (D64)   **comet** (D64)

As you read the summary, fill in the blanks with vocabulary terms.

An _____orbit_____ is the path an object takes as it moves

around another object in space. A _____planet_____ is a large body
of rock or gas that orbits the sun. There are nine planets in the

_____solar system_____. Earth is one of those planets. The sun is the
center of the solar system. It is a star made of hot, glowing gases. The

sun is closer to Earth than other stars are. _____Asteroids_____

and _____comets_____ are also parts of the solar system.

Follow the directions for each question.

1. List three ways that Earth is different from the other inner planets.
It has a watery surface; it is the only planet with a lot of oxygen in the
atmosphere; and it has plant and animal life.

2. List three ways the outer planets are alike. Answers may include any
three of the following: They are made mostly of frozen gases; they
are very far from the sun so their surfaces are much colder than the
inner planets; they are much larger than the inner planets; most have
many moons; and many have rings of dust and ice around them.

Harcourt

How Sunlight Strikes Earth

Materials

clear tape

large book

meterstick

wooden block

graph paper

flashlight

black marker

red marker

Activity Procedure

1 Tape the graph paper to the book.

2 Hold the flashlight about 50 cm above the book. Shine the light straight down. The beam will make a circle on the paper. If the circle is bigger than the paper, bring the light closer.

3 Have a partner use the black marker to draw around the light beam on the paper.

4 **Observe** the brightness of the light on the squares. **Record** your observations.

5 Keep the flashlight in the same position. Have a partner put the block under one end of the book and use the red marker to draw around the light on the paper.

6 **Observe** the brightness on the squares again. **Record** your observations.

Harcourt

Name _____

Draw Conclusions

1. How many squares are inside the black line? How many squares are inside the red line? _The answers will depend on size of the graph paper squares and the distance of the light from the paper. However, there should be more squares inside the red line than inside the black line._

2. Inside which line was the light brighter? _The light should have looked brighter inside the black line._

3. **Scientists at Work** Scientists **compare** things to find out how they are the same and how they are different. Compare the results of Steps 3 and 5 of the investigation. Do straight light rays or tilted light rays give stronger light? Suppose the paper is Earth's surface. The light is the sun.

Which area would have warmer weather? Explain. _Straight rays; the area inside the black line would have warmer weather because the light is brighter inside these squares._

Investigate Further Form a hypothesis about what will happen if the book is tilted even more. **Plan and conduct an experiment** to test your

hypothesis. _Tilting the book will make the rays more slanted. The light will be less strong._

Harcourt

Name _____

Date _____

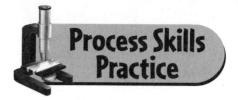

Compare

When you compare, you observe the properties of two or more things to see how they are alike and how they are different.

Think About Comparing

In September, Jean hung a picture of her favorite gymnast on the wall of her room. She hung it in a spot where the sun would shine on it at 3:00 P.M. each day, just when she sat down to do her homework. One day Jean noticed that the sun wasn't shining on her picture anymore. It was shining on her wall next to the picture. Jean thought this was interesting. She taped a circle of paper on the wall where the sun shone. She put the date and time on the paper. The next week, the sun was shining lower on the wall. She taped another circle of paper where the sun shone. Once a week she saw the sunny spot was lower on the wall and taped a circle of paper where the sun shone. She put the time and date on each circle of paper. By January 1, Jean had 16 circles of paper taped to her wall.

1. What did Jean observe about the sunny spot? She observed that the
sunny spot was moving as the days went by.

2. What two things could Jean compare? where the sunny spot was at
the beginning of September and where it was for each of the next
16 weeks

3. How else could Jean record her observations and comparisons?
Make a chart to record the date of each observation and the
distance the spot had moved from the previous week. Accept all
reasonable answers.

4. What could Jean infer from her observations? The relative positions of
her room and the sun were constantly changing. Accept any
reasonable answer.

Harcourt

Use with page D67.

Name _____

Date _____

Use Graphic Sources for Information

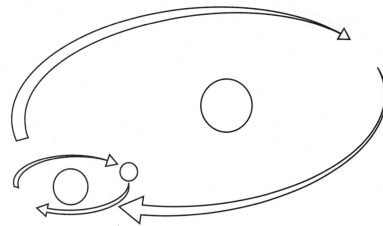

"Both Earth and the moon rotate. Earth rotates once a day. The moon rotates about once a month."

Write *True* or *False* next to each statement. If the statement is false, rewrite it to make it true.

1. Earth revolves around the sun.

True
_____

_____

2. The sun revolves around the moon.

False. The moon revolves around Earth.
_____

_____

3. Earth and the moon both revolve around the sun.

True
_____

_____

4. The moon remains still as it revolves around the Earth.

False. The moon rotates on its axis as it revolves around Earth.
_____

_____

Harcourt

What Causes Earth's Seasons?

Lesson Concept

Earth has seasons because its axis is tilted. This means the sun heats Earth's surface differently at different times of the year.

Vocabulary

rotation (D68)   **axis** (D68)   **revolution** (D68)

Underline the correct answer.

1. Earth rotates. Rotation is ____.

  A a revolution   **B** the spinning of an   **C** a season
                            object on its axis

2. Earth makes revolutions around the sun. Earth's revolution takes ____.

  A one year   **B** a lunar year   **C** three months in
                                              summer

3. Earth's axis is tilted. If Earth's axis were not tilted there would be ____.

  A only three   **B** seasons every   **C** no seasons
     seasons   other year

4. Seasons in the northern and southern halves of Earth are ____.

  A reversed   **B** the same   **C** moving

5. For part of the year, the North Pole points in the direction of the sun. This occurs during ____ in the Northern Hemisphere.

  A winter   **B** winter and   **C** summer
                     summer

Harcourt

The Moon's Phases

Materials

lamp with no shade

softball

Activity Procedure

1 Work with a partner. Turn on the lamp. Your teacher will darken the room.

2 Have person 1 hold the ball and stand with his or her back to the lighted bulb. Hold the ball as shown on page D75. Continue holding the ball this way until the end of the procedure.

3 Have person 2 stand in position 1. **Observe** the ball. Make a drawing of the ball's lighted side.

4 Person 2 now moves to position 2. Turn toward the ball. Make a drawing of the lighted part of the ball.

5 Have person 2 move to position 3. Make a drawing of the lighted part of the ball.

6 Person 2 again moves, this time to position 4. Turn toward the ball. Make a drawing of the lighted part of the ball.

7 Switch roles and repeat the procedure so person 1 can observe the patterns of light on the ball.

Harcourt

Name _____

Draw Conclusions

1. What part of the ball was lighted at each position? Position 1—all of
the ball is lighted; Position 2—half is lighted; Position 3—none is
lighted; Position 4—the other half of the ball is lighted.

_____

2. The ball represents the moon. What does the light bulb represent? What
represents a person viewing the moon from Earth? the sun, the person
doing the drawing

_____

3. **Scientists at Work** Scientists **use models** to make **inferences** to explain
how things work. If the ball represents the moon, what can you infer that
the different parts of the lighted ball represent? the phases of the moon

_____

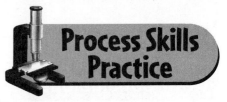

Process Skills Practice

Observe and Infer

When you observe, you use your senses to gather information.

Think About Observing and Inferring

One night Isaac looked out his window and saw a big moon in the sky. He wanted to get some information about the moon by observing it. He went out every night to see how the moon had changed. He drew a picture each night for four weeks. Every night he saw a small change in how the moon looked. He made notes about what he observed. Here are some of the notes Isaac made.

OCT. 5 BIG, BIG MOON
OCT. 12 MOON LOOKS HALF GONE
OCT. 15 NOW ITS EVEN SMALLER, LESS THAN HALF
OCT. 18 A LITTLE, TINY, SLIVER

1. What observations did he make of the moon? The moon was big when he first started observing; it seemed to change shape; it got smaller over the days.

2. How could Isaac learn more about the moon through observations? He could watch the moon for a longer period to see if the changes were the same each month; he could watch at different times of the year to see if anything was different; he could work with a partner and see if they both came up with the same drawings.

3. What inference could you make about why the moon looked different over the time period of Isaac's observations? Students should infer that the moon may be moving (phases of the moon).

Harcourt

Name _____

Date _____

Identify Cause and Effect

Earth, Moon, and Sun

Underline the causes and circle the effects in the following sentences.

1. When the sun shines on an object, the object casts a shadow.

2. When Earth's shadow falls on the moon, a lunar eclipse happens.

3. A total lunar eclipse makes all of the moon's face look dark red.

4. A solar eclipse happens when the moon's shadow falls on Earth.

5. When a total eclipse occurs, the whole sky turns dark in the middle of the day.

Identify the cause and effect shown in the picture.

Cause: _The sun came out and shone on the house._

Effect: _The house cast a shadow._

Use with page D78.

Harcourt

How Do the Moon and Earth Interact?

Lesson Concept

Phases are the different shapes the moon seems to have in the sky.
The moon goes through its phases every $29\frac{1}{2}$ days.

Vocabulary

phase (D76)   **lunar eclipse** (D78)   **solar eclipse** (D80)

As you read the summary, fill in each blank with a vocabulary term.

The half of the moon that faces the sun is always lighted. As the moon
moves around Earth, different parts of its lighted and dark sides face Earth.
The moon's phase depends on the part of the lighted half that can be seen.
The different shapes the moon seems to have in the sky are called
_____phases_____. There are solar and lunar eclipses. A ___solar eclipse___.
happens when the moon's shadow falls on Earth. A ___lunar eclipse___
happens when Earth's shadow falls on the moon.

Circle the term that best completes the sentence.

1. The half of the moon that faces the sun is always _____.
 A dark   (**B** lighted)

2. _____ are the different shapes the moon seems to have.
 (**A** Phases)   **B** Rotations

3. A lunar eclipse happens when Earth's _____ falls on the moon.
 (**A** shadow)   **B** atmosphere

4. The moon's shadow falling on Earth is the cause of a _____ eclipse.
 (**A** solar)   **B** lunar

Harcourt

Name _____

Date _____

Recognize Vocabulary

The vocabulary terms that follow are not correctly defined.
Write the correct meaning for each term.

1. **solar system**—the moon and objects that revolve around it

   the sun and objects that revolve around it
   _____

   _____

2. **orbit**—the path of the sun the path an object takes as it moves
   _____
   around another object in space

   _____

3. **planet**—a large body of fire that orbits the sun a large body of rock or
   _____
   gas that orbits the sun

   _____

4. **asteroid**—a shooting star a chunk of rock or metal that orbits the sun
   _____

   _____

   _____

5. **comet**—a large ball of dust and ice that orbits the moon

   a large ball of dust and ice that orbits the sun
   _____

   _____

6. **rotation**—the spinning of an object in space the spinning of an object
   _____
   on its axis

   _____

7. **Earth's axis**—an actual line that goes through the North and South Poles

   an imaginary line that goes through the North and South Poles

   _____

Harcourt

Name _____

Date _____

Explain a Solar Eclipse

Informative Writing–Explanation

Imagine that you are able to communicate with people living thousands of years ago. They ask you to explain what really happens during a solar eclipse. Write a simple explanation, and illustrate it with drawings. Use the outline below to help you plan your writing.

Words	Pictures
What causes a solar eclipse?	
What happens on Earth during a solar eclipse?	
In the beginning:	
At the peak of the eclipse:	
After the eclipse peaks:	
How can you stay safe during a solar eclipse?	

Harcourt

Use with pages D86–D87.

Properties of Matter

LESSON 1
PHYSICAL PROPERTIES

Three Physical Properties of Matter: Also accept: can or cannot be seen

1. size
2. color through, temperature,
3. shininess texture, taste, smell, and so on.

Three States of Matter:

4. solid: has a definite volume and shape
5. liquid: has a definite volume but shape can change
6. gas: has no definite shape or volume

LESSON 2
SOLIDS, LIQUIDS, AND GASES

1. Matter is made of atoms .

Changing States of Matter

2. Adding heat changes a solid to a liquid .

3. Adding heat changes a liquid to a gas .

4. Taking away heat from a gas changes it to a liquid .

5. Taking away heat from a liquid changes it to a solid .

LESSON 3
MEASURING MATTER

1. The amount of space that matter takes up is its volume .

2. The amount of matter in an object is its mass .

Harcourt

Name _____

Date _____

Physical Properties

Materials

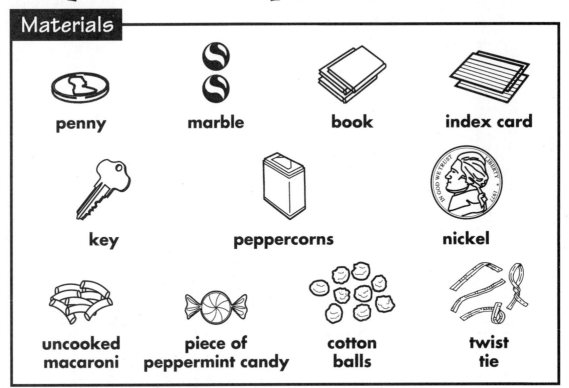

penny   marble   book   index card

key   peppercorns   nickel

uncooked macaroni   piece of peppermint candy   cotton balls   twist tie

Activity Procedure

1 Make charts like those on the next page.

2 Look at the objects you have been given. Notice whether they look shiny or dull. Notice how many colors each one has. **Record** your **observations**.

3 Touch the objects. Feel whether the objects are hard or soft. Feel whether they are rough or smooth. **Record** your **observations**.

4 Next, tap each object lightly with your fingernail. What kind of sound does it make? **Record** your **observations**.

5 Smell each object. **Record** your **observations**.

Harcourt

Name _____

Object	How It Looks			How It Feels			
	Shiny	Dull	Color	Hard	Soft	Rough	Smooth

Object	How It Smells			How It Sounds			
	Sweet	Sharp	No Smell	Loud	Soft	Makes a Ping	No Sound

Draw Conclusions
Possible answers are given.

1. Which objects are hard and rough? penny, nickel, key, pepper

Which objects are hard and smooth? marble, candy, macaroni, book

Which objects are soft and rough? cotton balls

Which objects are soft and smooth? card, twist tie

2. Compare your chart with the chart of another group. Are any objects in different columns? Why? Students will probably not classify all objects the same way. Reasons will vary. Accept all reasonable answers.

_____

3. Scientists at Work Scientists learn about the world by **observing** with their five senses. Which of the five senses did you not use in the investigation? taste

Investigate Further form a hypothesis About how physical properties change with the size of the sample. **Plan and conduct an experiment** to test your hypothesis.

You may want to provide students with a copy of TR131. Students should make up a chart called It Tastes, with columns labeled as sweet, sour, salty, bitter, good, and bad. They should list foods from their lunches in the appropriate columns. Accept all reasonable answers.

Harcourt

Observe and Record

You use your senses to observe the world around you. As you
make observations, you can record your data by writing it down.

Think About Observing and Recording

Dmitri asked his friend Rosa, a chef, to give a talk at his kitchen supply store.
Rosa spoke to Dmitri's customers about preparing a meal properly. Rosa
told the customers that when she shops, she looks carefully at everything she
buys to be sure it is fresh. She lightly squeezes a package of bread to be sure
it is not hard and stale. Even while she is preparing the food, she continues
to observe it. When she washes the lettuce for salad, she feels it to be sure it
is crisp. After the food is cooked, Rosa tastes it to see if she needs to add salt.
She also looks at the food on the plate to be sure it looks good.

1. What senses does Rosa use to observe the food? sight, touch, and taste

   _____

2. How do Rosa's observations help her prepare a meal?
   Possible answer: Rosa's observations help her tell if the food is
   fresh and will taste good.

3. Suppose you had these foods for lunch. For each food, circle the
   observation to record what you would expect.

Food	Observation	
Peanut Butter	bitter	(salty)
Bread	(fresh)	stale
Celery	soft	(crunchy)
Cookies	sour	(sweet)

Harcourt

Name _____

Date _____

Compare and Contrast

Read about different kinds of matter in the following sentences. Then tell what is being compared in each sentence, and tell whether the things are alike or different.

Matter

1. Both a horse and a dog are made of matter, but a horse is much larger than a dog.
   What is being compared? _____ horse _____ and _____ dog _____
   Are they alike or different? _____ different _____

2. The fur on a slipper feels soft, but the sole is hard and smooth.
   What is being compared? _____ fur _____ and _____ sole _____
   Are they alike or different? _____ different _____

3. Putty and clay are both things that can bend.
   What is being compared? _____ putty _____ and _____ clay _____
   Are they alike or different? _____ alike _____

4. A skunk has an unpleasant odor, but a lilac usually has a nice scent.
   What is being compared? _____ skunk _____ and _____ lilac _____
   Are they alike or different? _____ different _____

Harcourt

What Are Physical Properties of Matter?

Lesson Concept

Matter has many physical properties that you can observe by using your five senses.

Vocabulary

matter (E6)	**physical property** (E6)	**solid** (E11)
gas (E12)	**liquid** (E12)	

Answer the following questions about matter.

1. John and Tony go to the circus. They see a lion, a giraffe, and an elephant.

   John, Tony, and the animals are matter because they ____A____.

   A take up space   **B** are breathing   **C** are at the circus

2. John and Tony observe a tall clown on stilts and a tiny clown riding a tricycle. One clown has pink hair. Another clown wears a very large fake nose. What physical properties do John and Tony observe with their

   sense of sight? __C__

   A smell and color   **B** taste and feel   **C** size and color

3. Tony smells something good. It's popcorn! Tony and John get bags of salty, buttery popcorn and cups of sweet pink lemonade. Taste and smell are physical properties of matter. Which words describe these senses?

   __C__

   A soft and fuzzy   **B** light and dark   **C** sweet and salty

4. John buys Tony helium balloons to take home from the circus. In which

   state of matter is the helium inside the balloon? __A__

   A gas   **B** solid   **C** liquid

Harcourt

One Way Matter Can Change

Materials

 clear plastic cup

 2 ice cubes

 paper towel

 marker

Activity Procedure

1 Place the plastic cup on the paper towel. Put the ice cubes in the cup.

2 **Form a hypothesis** about what will happen to the ice cubes after 45 minutes.

_____

_____

3 **Observe** what's in the cup after 45 minutes. **Record** what you see.

_____

Was your hypothesis correct? _____

4 Mark the outside of the cup to show how high the water is. **Predict** what you will see inside the cup in the morning if you leave it out all night. Then leave the cup sitting out.

My prediction: _____

_____

5 **Observe** the cup the next morning. **Record** what you see.

_____

_____

Harcourt

Name _____

Draw Conclusions

1. What do you think caused the ice to change? The warm temperature in
the room caused the ice to melt.

_____

2. What do you think happened to the water when you left it out all night?
The warmth in the classroom caused some of the water to
become a gas.

_____

3. Scientists at Work Scientists form **hypotheses** based on things they have **observed** before. What had you observed before that helped you make your predictions? Answers will vary. Students should realize
that they rely on their personal experiences to predict future events.

_____

Investigate Further Plan and conduct an experiment to test this **hypothesis:** water freezes faster than orange juice. _____
The water freezes before the orange juice.

_____

Harcourt

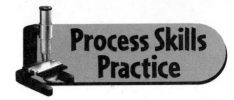

Process Skills Practice

Hypothesize

Read the paragraph below. Make a hypothesis about what might happen next.

Winter Pond

As winter comes and the temperature drops, the water in the pond changes from one state to another. When the temperature drops below 0°C (32° F), the water changes from liquid water to solid ice. It will stay ice until the temperature rises above 0°C.

What will happen to the water when spring comes? Write your hypothesis on the lines below.

Possible hypothesis: When the temperature rises above freezing, the

ice in the pond will warm up and change from a solid (ice) to a liquid

(water).

Name _____

Date _____

Use Prefixes and Suffixes to Determine Word Meaning

A prefix or a suffix can change the meaning of a word. For each root word below, add the suffixes from the list in each box. Write whether the new word is a noun or a verb. Then write a definition for each new word.

Suffixes	
-ion the word becomes a noun	
-ing the word becomes part of a verb	

1. Root word: evaporate

new word: evaporation

noun or verb: noun

definition: the act of evaporating, or of a liquid becoming a gas

new word: evaporating

noun or verb: verb

definition: changing from a liquid to a gas

2. Root word: connect

new word: connection

noun or verb: noun

definition: the act of becoming connected or joined

new word: connecting

noun or verb: verb

definition: becoming joined or connected

Harcourt

What Are Solids, Liquids, and Gases?

Lesson Concept

Atoms are small particles that make up matter. Whether matter is a solid, liquid, or gas depends on how tightly atoms fit together.

Vocabulary

atom (E16)   **evaporation** (E18)

Put a check mark in front of the statement in each pair that agrees with what you have learned.

____✓____ **1.** The atoms of solids do not move very much.

_____ The atoms of solids can slide past each other.

_____ **2.** Gas particles stick together tightly.

____✓____ Gas particles are not connected to each other and are not close to each other.

____✓____ **3.** Particles of liquid are more loosely attached than those in a solid. The particles can slide past each other.

_____ Particles of liquid are like those in a solid.

____✓____ **4.** The state of matter can be changed by adding or taking away heat.

_____ The state of matter can be changed by touching the particles.

_____ **5.** Gas particles are the basic building blocks of matter.

____✓____ Atoms are the basic building blocks of matter.

Harcourt

Name _____

Date _____

Measuring Mass and Volume

Materials

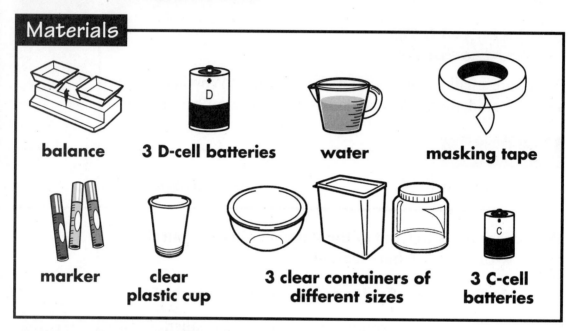

balance   3 D-cell batteries   water   masking tape

marker   clear plastic cup   3 clear containers of different sizes   3 C-cell batteries

Activity Procedure

Part A

1 Put a C-cell in the pan on the left side of the balance. Put a D-cell in the pan on the right side. **Record** which battery is heavier.

2 Add C-cells to the left side and D-cells to the right side until the pans are balanced. You may need to use some of the small masses from the balance to make the cells balance perfectly. **Record** the number of C-cells and D-cells you use.

Part B

3 Fill the cup half-full with water. Use a piece of tape to mark how high the water is in the cup. **Predict** how high the water will be in each container if you pour the water into it. Mark each prediction with a piece of tape. Write P (for prediction) on the tape.

4 Pour the water into the next container. Mark the height of the water with a piece of tape. Write *A* (for *Actual*) on the tape.

Harcourt

Investigate Log

5 Repeat Step 4 for each of the other containers.

Draw Conclusions

1. **Compare** the numbers of C-cells and D-cells it took to balance the pans. **Draw a conclusion** from these numbers about the masses of the batteries.

   It takes two C-cells to balance one D-cell. D-cells have more

   mass than C-cells.

   _____

2. Describe the height of the water in each container. Why did the same amount of water look different in the different containers?

   The water looked as if it took up different amounts of space in

   different containers. The same amount of liquid would look like less

   in a short, wide container than in a tall, thin container.

   _____

   _____

3. **Scientists at Work** Scientists **measure** matter by using tools that are marked with standard amounts. What was the standard amount you used in this activity to measure the water? _a cup half-full of water_

   _____

Harcourt

Name _____

Date _____

Process Skills Practice

Measure

Measuring is a way to observe and compare things accurately. You can use an instrument like a ruler or a balance to measure the size of an object.

Think About Measuring

Tina brought two boxes of cookies to class. One box was larger than the other. She invited three classmates to look at the boxes and predict which had more mass. Two classmates chose the larger box. She put the two boxes on the balance. Look at the picture.

1. What does the balance show about the two boxes of cookies?

Even though they look different from each other, the boxes have the same mass.

Tina also brought juice to share equally with her group. But none of the glasses she brought were the same size. Before she poured the juice, Tina wanted to be sure each classmate had the same amount. For each classmate, she used a measuring cup and measured 1 cup. Then she poured the juice into a glass. She noticed that the level of the juice was different in all the glasses.

12-oz glass   **15-oz glass**   **20-oz glass**

2. Why was it a good idea that Tina measured the juice in a measuring cup before pouring it into each glass? Accept reasonable answers.

Students should show that they understand it is hard to compare the amount of juice in two glasses if the glasses are different shapes and sizes.

Harcourt

Name _____

Date _____

Distinguish Fact and Opinion

Write whether each sentence is a fact or an opinion.

1. The same volume of liquid may look different in different containers.

fact
_____

2. Using measuring cups is the best way to measure liquids.

opinion
_____

3. Softballs are heavy.

opinion
_____

4. A golf ball has more mass than a Ping Pong ball.

fact
_____

5. The dog weighs 8 kilograms (about 18 lb).

fact
_____

6. When you cut an apple into halves, you still have the same amount of mass.

fact
_____

7. Apples are the best fruit for snacking because they have a lot of mass.

opinion
_____

8. Measuring apples is easy if you know how to do it.

opinion
_____

9. A balance accurately measures mass.

fact
_____

10. All scientists use balances.

opinion
_____

Harcourt

How Can Matter Be Measured?

Lesson Concept

Volume is the amount of space an object takes up. Mass is how much matter is in an object. Different objects can have the same volume but different masses.

Vocabulary

volume (E22)   **mass** (E24)

Put a check mark in front of the statement in each pair that agrees with what you have learned.

_____ **1.** The amount of space matter takes up is called mass.

__✓___ The amount of space matter takes up is called volume.

_____ **2.** You can tell how much mass an object has just by looking at it.

__✓___ You can measure an object to tell how much mass it has.

_____ **3.** Mass is the amount of liquid in an object.

__✓___ Mass is the amount of matter in an object.

_____ **4.** Air is a gas that cannot be seen and has no mass.

__✓___ Air and other gases have mass.

__✓___ **5.** Different kinds of matter can take up the same amount of space but have different masses.

_____ If different kinds of matter take up the same amount of space, they have the same mass.

Harcourt

Vocabulary Review

Recognize Vocabulary

Match each term in Column A with its definition in Column B.

Column A

_____ **1.** It does not have a definite shape or a definite volume.

_____ **2.** They are the basic building blocks of matter.

_____ **3.** This is the process in which a liquid becomes a gas.

_____ **4.** This is the amount of space matter takes up.

_____ **5.** It is anything you can observe about an object by using your senses.

_____ **6.** All matter has volume and _____ .

_____ **7.** It is anything that takes up space.

_____ **8.** It takes up a specific amount of space and has a definite shape.

_____ **9.** It has a volume that stays the same, but it can change its shape.

Column B

A mass

B volume

C evaporation

D solid

E matter

F atoms

G physical property

H liquid

I gas

Harcourt

Name _____

Date _____

Tell How to Check Volume

Informative Writing—How-to

Everyone on the soccer team was asked to bring two liters of water to the game. Each player brought the water in a different size and shape of container. No one brought a measuring cup, but one player brought the water in a 2-liter bottle. Write a set of steps for checking whether each player brought the right amount of water. Do not use a measuring cup. Use the outline below to plan your writing.

Step 1:

Step 2:

Step 3:

Step 4:

Harcourt

Chapter 2 • Graphic Organizer for Chapter Concepts

Changes in Matter

LESSON 1
PHYSICAL CHANGES

Ways Matter Can Change Physically and Still Be the Same Matter

1. shape _____

2. size _____

3. state _____

Ways To Physically Mix Matter

1. mixture _____

2. solution _____

LESSON 2
CHEMICAL CHANGES

During a chemical change, new matter is formed _____.

Examples of Chemical Changes

1. burning _____

2. rust _____

How Chemical Changes Are Used

1. cook food _____

2. plants make food _____

3. film changes to make photographs _____

Harcourt

Separate a Mixture

Materials

4 clear plastic cups

6 marbles

water

steel paper clips

rice

magnet

measuring cup

paper towels

funnel

Activity Procedure

1 In one cup, make a mixture of marbles and water. Plan a way to separate the marbles from the water. Try it. **Record** your method and your results.

My method: _____

My results: _____

2 In another cup, make a mixture of marbles, paper clips, and rice. Plan a way to separate the mixture. Try it. **Record** your method and your results.

My method: _____

My results: _____

Harcourt

Name _____

3 If your method doesn't work, plan a different way to separate the mixture. Try different methods until you find one that works. Try using the magnet. **Record** each method you try and your results.

My method: _____

My results: _____

4 In another cup, mix $\frac{1}{4}$ cup of rice with 1 cup of water. How could you separate the rice from the water? **Record** your ideas.

My ideas: _____

5 Make a filter with the paper towels and the funnel. **Predict** how this tool could be used to separate the mixture. Then use the filter to separate the mixture.

My prediction: _____

Draw Conclusions

1. When would it be easy to use only your hands to separate a mixture?
Using your hands works only when the mixture is made up of large, solid pieces.

2. When might you need a tool to separate a mixture? A tool is useful when some pieces are very small or there are solids and liquids together.

3. **Scientists at Work** Scientists often use charts to **record** the results of an investigation. How would setting up charts help you **plan and conduct an experiment**? Answers will vary but may include a chart that could prevent students from repeating methods that didn't work.

_____

Investigate Further Make a mixture of sand and water. **Plan and conduct an experiment** to separate the mixture. Would a tool be useful? Yes.

Which tool would you use? a filter

Harcourt

Plan and Conduct an Experiment

You plan and conduct an experiment to find the answer to a
question or to solve a problem.

Think About Planning and Conducting an Experiment

Trey mistakenly dumped a large bag of flour into
the kitchen rice container. He planned and
conducted two experiments testing ways to separate
the mixture. He recorded the results of
his experiments.

Experiment #1 Made a small mixture of flour and rice in a jar. Picked the rice out, piece by piece. Result: Took too long. Was not a good method.	**Experiment #2** Made a small mixture of flour and rice in a jar. Used a strainer set over a bowl. Poured mixture into strainer. Result: Flour went through the strainer into bowl. Rice stayed in strainer. Good method for separating the mixture.

1. Why didn't the first experiment work? _It took too long to separate_
the mixture.

2. Why did Trey try two experiments before attempting to separate the

large mixture in his kitchen? _He wanted to find the best method before_
he did a lot of unnecessary work.

3. What might have happened if he hadn't done the experiments?
Answers will vary but should indicate that Trey might have spilled the

mixture or spent more time fixing his mistake than he needed to.

Arrange Events in Sequence

The following sets of sentences are out of order. Rewrite the sentences in each set so that they are in the correct sequence.

Physical Changes in Matter

The sun melted Jane's ice cream.
Jane left the bowl of ice cream outside on a warm day.
The ice cream became liquid.
Jane placed a scoop of ice cream in a bowl.

Jane placed a scoop of ice cream in a bowl.

Jane left the bowl of ice cream outside on a warm day.

The sun melted Jane's ice cream.

The ice cream became liquid.

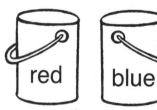

The paint turned purple.
Lou wanted to make purple paint.
He stirred the two colors together.
Lou poured blue paint into red paint.

Lou wanted to make purple paint.

Lou poured blue paint into red paint.

He stirred the two colors together.

The paint turned purple.

Harcourt

Concept Review

What Are Physical Changes?

Lesson Concept

Physical changes don't form new kinds of matter.

Vocabulary

physical changes (E40) **mixture** (E41) **solution** (E42)

Write the letter of the best answer on the lines.

1. In winter the pond water freezes. People skate on the ice. When the
   water freezes, ___C___.
   A new matter is formed   **C** the matter is the same matter
   B the matter becomes a mixture **D** the matter becomes a solution

2. A young girl cut a sheet of paper into paper dolls. The paper has gone
   through a ___A___.
   A physical change   **B** matter change   **C** state change

3. Emily poured raisins, apple slices, and cinnamon into a bowl. She stirred
   them together. The raisins, apple slices, and cinnamon are ___B___.
   A a solution   **B** a mixture   **C** a condensation

4. A glass of lemonade was left out in the backyard. After a few days, only
   the sugar remained. What separated the solution? ___B___
   A condensation   **B** evaporation   **C** precipitation

5. A solution is a kind of mixture that ___C___.
   A cannot be eaten   **B** cannot freeze   **C** cannot be separated
                                                        by hand

Harcourt

Chemical Changes

Materials

safety goggles

cookie sheet

large glass bowl

measuring cup

baking soda

vinegar

 CAUTION ## Activity Procedure

1 **CAUTION** Put on your safety goggles.

2 Place the cookie sheet on the table. Place the bowl on the cookie sheet.

3 **Measure** $\frac{1}{4}$ cup of baking soda. Pour it into the bowl.

4 **Measure** $\frac{1}{4}$ cup of vinegar. Hold the cup with the vinegar in one hand. Use your other hand to fan some of the air from the cup toward your nose. Do not put your nose directly over the cup.

5 Pour the vinegar into the bowl.

6 **Observe** the matter in the bowl. **Record** what it looks like. Use the procedure from Step 4 to smell the matter in the bowl. Record what it smells like.

What it looks like: _____

_____

What it smells like: _____

_____

Harcourt

Name _____

Draw Conclusions

1. How is the material in the bowl like the baking soda and vinegar you started with? The solid material is white like the baking soda.

How is it different? The material doesn't smell like vinegar.

2. What can you **infer** about where the bubbles came from?

Accept all reasonable guesses. The bubbles were made by a gas

(CO_2) that formed as a result of the chemical reaction. The gas then

mixed with the air.

3. **Scientists at Work** Scientists **observe** changes. Then they **record** their observations. Describe the changes you observed in the bowl.

Answers will vary, but students should describe the bubbles

that formed.

Investigate Further Mix warm water and a fresh packet of dry yeast. **Observe** the mixture. **Record** what you see. What can you **infer** about the changes you see? Bubbles form. The bubbles that formed when vinegar

was mixed with baking soda meant that a gas had formed. The bubbles

that form here also mean a gas has formed.

Harcourt

Observe and Infer

You use your senses to observe the world around you. When you infer, you use your observations to form an opinion.

Think About Observing and Inferring

Tasha had some pennies that looked dull and were brown colored. She wanted to find out what the pennies looked like when they were new. She put on safety goggles. She put the pennies in a jar. Then she added 1 cup of vinegar. She noticed the strong smell of the vinegar. She saw that the pennies were not fully covered, so she poured in more vinegar. After 15 minutes she looked in the jar. The pennies were now bright and shiny. They were copper colored just as they were when they were new. The vinegar was dark colored.

1. Why was it important for Tasha to wear safety goggles when she did the experiment? The vinegar could splash into her eyes and harm them.

2. What senses did Tasha use in this experiment, and how did she use them?
She used sight to look at the pennies; she used smell to smell the vinegar.

3. What observations did Tasha make about the pennies and the vinegar after the experiment was completed? The pennies were bright and copper colored, and the vinegar was dark.

4. What can you infer about what changed the color of the pennies?
Accept reasonable answers. Students should connect the application of vinegar with the change of color. Some students may suspect that vinegar removed an old coating on the pennies.

Harcourt

Name _____

Date _____

Summarize and Paraphrase a Selection

Chemical Changes at Home

Many kinds of chemical changes can occur in the home every day. A chemical change happens when you bake a cake. When someone eats the cake, chemical changes happen in the body. One occurs when saliva in the mouth mixes with the food. Some of the starches in the food are changed to sugar. The burning of fuel is a chemical change. A furnace may burn oil to heat a home. When wood is burned in the fireplace, a new kind of matter called ash is formed. Rusting is a chemical change. Iron nails that have been exposed to air and water can rust. Chemical changes called photosynthesis occur in plants when they make their own food.

1. What is the main idea of the paragraph?

Many kinds of chemical changes can occur in the home

every day.

_____

2. What are six examples that support the main idea?

baking a cake

eating cake

burning oil

burning wood

rusting

photosynthesis

Harcourt

Use with page E47.

What Are Chemical Changes?

Lesson Concept

Chemical changes cause new kinds of matter to form.

Vocabulary

chemical changes (E46)

Use a word from the list below to complete each of the following statements.

matter	physical	rusting

1. The kind of matter stays the same in _____ physical _____ changes.

2. _____ Rusting _____ is a chemical change that damages metal.

3. In a chemical change, the particles of matter change to form a new kind of _____ matter _____.

Answer the questions below.

1. Explain why burning wood is a chemical change.

   When things burn, different kinds of matter form. Wood combines with oxygen to form a new kind of matter: smoke and ash.

2. What are some chemical changes that you notice in your daily life? Answers will vary. Students may mention cooking food, burning fuel for heat, taking pictures, burning wood in the fireplace, and so on.

Harcourt

Recognize Vocabulary

Write the letter of the correct answer in the blank.

1. In a chemical change, two kinds of matter combine to form _____. *A*

    A a different kind of matter   **B** a mixture

2. After a physical change, _____. *B*

    A new matter is formed   **B** matter often looks different

3. A mixture is a substance that contains _____. *B*

    A only one type of matter   **B** two or more types of matter

4. A solution is a mixture of _____. *A*

    A different kinds of particles mixed together evenly   **B** some particles that are mixed together and some that stay apart

Put a check mark on the lines of the paragraphs that talk about chemical changes.

✓ **1.** The Sinclair family is celebrating Jacob Sinclair's fifth birthday with a camping trip. Before they go, Jacob's mother makes cupcakes. She mixes together flour, milk, eggs, butter, and chocolate. She puts the cupcakes in the oven to bake. When they are done, she frosts them.

_____ **2.** Next, Mrs. Sinclair makes a piñata. She cuts up paper and soaks the paper in glue. Then she forms the paper into the shape of a cow. She stuffs the piñata with candy.

✓ **3.** At the campsite that night, the Sinclair family builds a fire in the fire pit. First, the wooden logs go in, and then the fire is lighted. The logs burn brightly, smoke rises in the air, and ashes fall from the burned wood.

✓ **4.** The next morning the family gets ready to go home. They gather up all the trash. They throw the food scraps into a special container and mix them all together. Then they get in the car to drive home.

Harcourt

Name _____

Date _____

Compare Combinations

Informative Writing—Compare and Contrast

Write a paragraph about mixtures and suspensions. Give an example of each of these combinations of matter. Tell how they are alike and how they are different. Use the Venn diagram below to help you plan your writing.

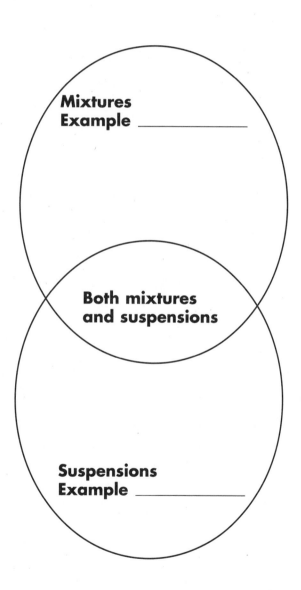

Mixtures
Example _____

Both mixtures
and suspensions

Suspensions
Example _____

Harcourt

Name _____ Date _____

Chapter 1 • Graphic Organizer for Chapter Concepts

Energy

LESSON 1
WHAT IS ENERGY?

```
comes
mainly from
the sun

needed by
living things
and by
machines                    energy                  can be
                                                    stored for
                                                    later use

                            found in
                            different                may be
                            forms                    described as
                                                     potential or
                                                     kinetic
```

LESSON 2
HOW DOES ENERGY MOVE?

Light

moves as up-and-down

_____

_____ waves

Sound

moves as back-and-forth

_____

_____ waves

Electricity

moves from batteries to

_____

_____ other objects

LESSON 3
HOW CAN ENERGY BE
CHANGED?

```
        sunlight

                    electricity ────→ light

          fuel

   food              motion
```

Harcourt

Name _____

Date _____

Twisting Up Energy

Materials

goggles

2 clothespins

1 rubber band

Activity Procedure

1 **CAUTION** Put on safety goggles to protect your eyes in case a clothespin pops loose.

2 Attach the rubber band to each clothespin. Work with a partner to twist the rubber band between the clothespins.

3 When you have finished, the rubber band should be twisted and curled up.

4 Holding the clothespins tightly, lay them on the table and **hypothesize** what will happen to them when you let them go. **Communicate** your hypothesis to your partner.

5 **Observe** what happens to the clothespins when you let them go. Then do the investigation again, this time twisting the pins more tightly than you did before. **Compare** what the clothespins did the first time with what they did the second time.

Harcourt

Name _____

Draw Conclusions

1. Describe what happened each time you put the clothespins on the table and let go of them. How did your hypothesis compare to the actual results? Students should report that the clothespins twisted around
each other as the rubber band unwound.

_____

2. Where did the energy to move the clothespins come from?
It came from the twisted rubber band, which got its energy from
the turning of the students' hands.

_____

3. Scientists at Work Scientists **conduct simple experiments** to learn more about how things work. What did you learn about energy and twisted rubber bands from your investigation? As they twist up,
the rubber bands store the energy students put in them. Then they
release the energy, as evidenced by the clothespins twisting on
the table.

Investigate Further Observe what happens to a third clothespin that you twist around the other two with a second rubber band.
Encourage students to hypothesize what will happen to the third
clothespin and to support their hypotheses.

_____

Harcourt

Name _____

Date _____

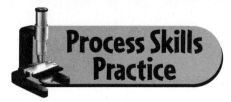

Hypothesize

When you hypothesize before conducting a simple investigation, you are explaining what you think will happen. Your hypothesis can be based on things you have observed, things you already know to be true, or things you have learned from earlier investigations.

Think About Hypothesizing

Harry has a windup toy. He noticed that when he winds it up six twists, it hops twelve times, on average. But when he winds it up three twists, it hops an average of six times. He developed a hypothesis: the toy will always hop twice the number of twists.

1. Where does the windup toy gets its energy? __from Harry's twists__

_____

2. How can Harry test his hypothesis? __He can do more tests with__
__different numbers of twists._____

3. How should Harry record his tests? __He should count the number__
__of twists and the number of hops and write them down. He could__
__make a chart or graph with his data.__

4. What if the results of his tests do not prove his hypothesis? What can he
do? __He can repeat the tests; look for reasons that the results are__
__different, such as a mistake in counting or a bumpy floor; or he can__
__form a new hypothesis and plan more investigations.__

5. If Harry looked inside the toy, what do you think he would find that
stores the energy? __probably a spring or a rubber band__

_____

Harcourt

Use with page F5.

Name _____

Date _____

Reading Skills
Practice

Compare and Contrast

Complete the chart below to compare how energy is used.

Two Things That Use or Produce Energy	How Are These Things Alike?	How Are These Things Different?
plants animals	Both use energy for food and growth.	Plants use energy to make their own food; animals eat food that contains stored energy.
electric heater fireplace	Both can warm a room.	The heater uses electricity to generate heat; the fireplace uses energy from burning wood or gas to generate heat.
cars people	Both use energy to move from one place to another.	Cars burn fuel; people use energy from the food they have eaten.
wood battery	Both use stored energy.	Wood uses stored energy from the sun; a battery uses stored energy from the chemicals that people have put into it.
food fossil fuel	Both are ways of storing energy.	Food is eaten by people and animals; fuel is burned to make heat, light, or electricity.

Harcourt

Concept Review

What Is Energy?

Lesson Concept

Energy is the ability to move something. All living things and machines need energy to function. Energy comes mainly from the sun, and can be found in many different forms. It can be stored and used later.

Vocabulary

energy (F6)   **electricity** (F7)   **fossil fuel** (F8)

potential energy (F6)   **kinetic energy** (F7)

Draw a line from each living thing or object in the left column to the source of the energy it uses in the right column.

1.

2.

3.

4.

5.

A

B

C

D

E

Name _____

Date _____

Waves of Energy

Materials

rope
about 6 feet long

coiled
spring toy

Activity Procedure

1 Do this investigation with a partner. Hold one end of the rope while your partner holds the other. Stand so that the rope hangs loosely between you.

2 While your partner holds his or her end of the rope still, move your end gently up and down. Now move the rope faster. **Compare** what the rope looked like before with what it looks like now.

3 Now take the coiled spring toy and place it on a table or on the floor. Hold one end, and have your partner hold the other.

4 Ask your partner to hold the end still as you quickly push your end of the toy in about 4 inches. Now push and pull your end backward and forward. **Observe** what happens to the coils.

5 Draw and label a diagram explaining what happened to the rope when you moved one end. Make another diagram showing what happened to the coiled spring toy when you pushed one end in.

Harcourt

Name _____

Draw Conclusions

1. What happened to the rope when you moved one end up and down? How did it move? What happened when you moved it faster?

   Possible answers: Waves formed along the rope, moving from one
   end to the other. When I moved it faster, more waves formed, they
   were closer together, and they went higher and higher.

2. What happened when you pushed your end of the coiled spring toy toward your partner? What happened when you moved it back and forth? Some of the coils bunched together and seemed to move from my side to my partner's side. When I pushed and pulled, lots of bunched coil sections moved back and forth.

3. **Scientists at Work** When things in nature can't be seen, scientists **use models** to see how they work. They then **communicate** what they learn. How did your diagram help you to communicate what you learned about how energy moves as waves? It showed in pictures and words what I learned.

Harcourt

Name _____

Date _____

Use Models and Communicate

You can use objects that you can see to model things that you cannot see. Then you can draw and label diagrams to communicate what you have learned. Models can include maps, pictures and diagrams, three-dimensional representations, and computer simulations.

Think About Using Models

We cannot see sounds, but if we observe carefully, we can see and feel the vibrations that make sounds happen. Observe the three pictures below.

1. What would you hear if you plucked the rubber band with your finger?

a twanging sound

2. How would the rubber band look while you were hearing the sound?

It would be vibrating rapidly.

3. If you placed a vibrating tuning fork into a bowl of water, what would you see?

The vibrations would make ripples in

the water.

4. Do sound waves travel through water?

yes

5. If you cover a comb with a piece of wax paper and then hum with your lips touching the wax paper, what would you feel?

vibrations

Harcourt

Use with page F15.

Reading Skills Practice

Use Prefixes and Suffixes to Determine Word Meaning

A word's meaning can be changed by adding a prefix or a suffix to the root word. Below is a list of root words and their definitions. Choose one prefix or one suffix from the box, and write the new word. Then write the definition of the new word.

prefixes	suffixes
re- un- pre-	-ing -tion -ity -ian

1. *move:* to change position from one point to another

prefix or suffix added: _____

new word: Possible new words: remove, removing

definition: Definitions will vary, depending on new word.

2. *vent:* to allow something to be released through an opening

prefix or suffix added: _____

new word: Possible new words: prevent, venting

definition: Definitions will vary, depending on new word.

3. *electric:* made of or powered by electricity

prefix or suffix added: _____

new word: Possible new words: electricity; electrician

definition: Definitions will vary, depending on new word.

4. *vibrate:* move back and forth very quickly

prefix or suffix added: _____

new word: Possible new words: vibrating, vibration

definition: Definitions will vary, depending on new word.

Harcourt

How Does Energy Move?

Lesson Concept

Energy can move in many different ways. Light energy moves as up-and-down waves. Sound energy moves as back-and-forth waves. Electricity moves from batteries to other objects. Thermal energy moves as heat and is transferred by touching or by radiation.

Vocabulary

vibrate (F19)   **circuit** (F20)

Read the sentence for clues to unscramble the term that belongs in the blank. Then rewrite the unscrambled term in the blank.

1. Sound energy and light move in _____ waves _____. **VSEAW**

2. Light travels _____ faster _____ than sound. **STREAF**

3. When you rub your hands together to get them warm, you make

   _____ thermal _____ energy. **MARETLH**

4. In a circuit, energy travels from the _____ battery _____ through the wires to the bulb. **RABYTET**

5. _____ Sound _____ vibrations can travel through liquids, solids, and gases. **ONDSU**

6. When you feel the thermal energy of hot cocoa in a cup, you are feeling

   _____ heat _____. **AETH**

7. Thermal energy that moves without touching anything is called

   _____ radiation _____. **AORIDINAT**

8. Fuel is a form of _____ stored _____ energy. **SEDTOR**

Harcourt

Name _____

Date _____

Lighting a Bulb

Materials

masking tape

D-cell battery

2 pieces of insulated electrical wire

miniature light bulb

Activity Procedure

1 Use a piece of masking tape to tape the battery to your desk. This way, it won't roll around.

2 As your partner holds the light bulb a few inches away from the battery, use the wires to connect the ends of the battery with the base of the bulb.

3 Now switch the wires. Do you **observe** any changes?

4 Try to make the bulb light by touching the wires to the glass part of the bulb. Can you make it light?

5 Can you make the bulb light by touching the wires to the sides of the battery?

Harcourt

Draw Conclusions

1. What happened when you connected the ends of the battery to the base of the light bulb by using the wires? _The bulb lit up._____

_____

2. What happened when you switched the wires? _The bulb still lit up.___

_____

3. Could you make the bulb light by touching the wires to the glass part of the bulb? Did the bulb light when you touched the wires to the sides of the battery? _no; no_____

4. Scientists at Work Scientists know that the results of experiments don't often turn out exactly the same every time. This can be caused by differences in materials or differences in procedure. How could you change the materials in this investigation to see if the results would change?

Possible answers: You could use different wire, bulb, or battery.

You could vary the length of the wires.

_____

_____

Investigate Further Plan and conduct a simple investigation to find out if you can make the bulb light by using something other than wires to connect the battery and the bulb. **Control variables** by using the same battery and bulb for each trial.

Materials that conduct electricity (most metals) will make the bulb light.

Insulators (plastic, cloth) will not.

_____

_____

Harcourt

Experiment and Draw Conclusions

When you do an experiment, you make a hypothesis. Then you gather data to test your hypothesis. You can observe and see evidence that helps you draw conclusions about why your hypothesis was—or was not—correct.

Think About Experimenting

In a circuit like the one in Diagram A, the light bulb will light. What do you think will happen if you add another battery to the circuit as in Diagram B?

Diagram A

Diagram B

1. Do you think the light bulb will light in the circuit shown in Diagram B?

yes

2. Do you think the light would be brighter in Diagram B? Explain your

answer. Yes, because two batteries give more energy than one.

_____

3. What do you think would happen if you added two more batteries to the

circuit? The light would get even brighter.

_____

Use Reference Sources

Use reference sources such as books, newspapers, magazines, or the Internet to write a paragraph or fact sheet about one of the topics below. List your reference sources and write your paragraph on this sheet.

Topics

1. Ways to Conserve Energy in the Home

2. How Greenhouses Help Plants Grow

3. How Windmills Are Used

4. How Solar Panels Work to Help Heat Homes

Your topic: _____

Reference sources used: _____

_____

_____

_____

_____

_____

_____

_____

_____

_____

_____

Harcourt

Concept Review

How Can Energy Be Changed?

Lesson Concept

Energy can change forms. Sunlight can become food, fuel, or electricity. Electricity can become other kinds of energy, such as light, heat, and motion. Food and fuel can become motion and heat.

Vocabulary

waste heat (F26)

Number these pictures in the correct sequence to show how energy is converted into different forms.

3

5

2

4

1

Harcourt

Recognize Vocabulary

In the space provided, write the letter of the term in column B that best fits the definition in column A. Use each term only once.

Column A

_C_ **1.** The ability to cause change

_J_ **2.** Where the energy in food comes from

_H_ **3.** A form of energy that travels through space as up-and-down waves

_E_ **4.** A form of energy that travels through material as back-and-forth waves

_B_ **5.** The type of energy found in food and fuel

_A_ **6.** The kind of energy that powers your refrigerator and your hair dryer

_I_ **7.** The path electricity follows

_F_ **8.** Fuel formed from organisms that lived millions of years ago

Column B

A electricity

B potential energy

C energy

D waste heat

E sound

F fossil fuel

G vibrate

H light

I circuit

J the sun

K kinetic energy

Choose two of the vocabulary terms from column B. Then, using your own words, write a sentence that uses each term correctly.

_____

_____

_____

_____

Harcourt

Name _____

Date _____

Tell a Story About Energy

Narrative Writing—Story

Tell the story of the gasoline that your family car or school bus runs on. Tell where it came from and what happened to the original matter through each step. Complete the sentences in the outline below to help you plan your writing.

Long ago, dinosaurs . . .

Decayed matter from dead dinosaurs . . .

Over time, the decayed matter was changed into . . .

Oil and gas companies dug wells in the ground to get . . .

In the car or bus engine, the gasoline . . .

Harcourt

Chapter 2 • Graphic Organizer for Chapter Concepts

Heat

LESSON 1
HEAT

What Is Heat?
Heat is the energy of the motion

of the particles in matter.

How to Make Things Hot
1. rub things together (friction)

2. burn things

3. mix chemicals together

Three Ways We Use Heat
1. heating homes

2. heating water

3. cooking

LESSON 2
THERMAL ENERGY
ON THE MOVE

Ways Thermal Energy Can Move
1. conduction

2. convection

3. radiation

Moving Through Materials
1. moves easily through a
conductor

2. can't move easily through an
insulator

LESSON 3
TEMPERATURE

How Thermal Energy Is Measured
thermometer

**How Humans Control
Thermal Energy**
1. wear clothes

2. thermostats

Harcourt

Name _____

Date _____

Rubbing Objects Together

Materials

metal button

small piece of wool

penny

sheet of paper

Activity Procedure

1 Hold your bare hands together, palms touching. Do your hands feel cold, hot, sticky, or damp? **Record** what you **observe**.

2 Make a **hypothesis**. What would you feel if you rubbed your hands together? **Record** your hypothesis.

3 Now rub your palms together very fast for about ten seconds. **Record** what you **observe**.

4 What might you feel if you rubbed the button with the wool? The penny with paper? Form a **hypothesis** for each test. **Record** each one.

5 Rub the button with the wool for about ten seconds. Touch the button. Touch the wool. **Record** what you **observe**.

6 Then rub the penny with the paper for about ten seconds. Touch the penny. Touch the paper. **Record** what you **observe**.

Harcourt

Name _____

Draw Conclusions

1. What changes did you **observe**? What actions did you perform that caused the changes you observed? The objects got warm. I rubbed one item against another.

   _____

2. Were your **hypotheses** correct? If not, how could you change them based on what you learned? Emphasize to students that many hypotheses are incorrect. When they are, the hypotheses are rewritten and retested. Students' answers will vary.

3. **Scientists at Work** Scientists use their knowledge and experiences to help them **hypothesize**. What knowledge and experiences did you use in this investigation to help you hypothesize? Answers will vary. Some students may have had experiences rubbing their hands together on a cold day to warm them up.

Harcourt

Hypothesize

When you hypothesize, you say what you think will happen if
something else happens.

Think About Hypothesizing

Lisa went to science class and read these two statements on the board:

1. Bend a piece of wire back and forth five or six times. After you bend
   it, you will notice that the bend in the wire feels cool.

2. Bend a piece of wire back and forth five or six times. After you bend
   it, you will notice that the bend in the wire feels warm.

One of the statements was wrong. To find out which hypothesis was wrong,
Lisa did an experiment: She took a piece of stiff wire about 30 centimeters
(12 in.) long. She felt the wire. It felt cool. She bent the wire back and forth
about five or six times. Then she felt the bend in the wire. The bend in the
wire felt warm.

1. Draw a line under the first hypothesis. What does it state about the bend
in the wire? _that the bend in the wire will be cool_____

_____

2. Draw a line under the second hypothesis. What does it state about the
bend in the wire? _that the bend in the wire will be warm_____

_____

3. Which hypothesis is correct? Why is it correct? _The second hypothesis___
_is correct. The wire felt warm after being bent._____

_____

Arrange Events in Sequence

Rewrite the following words and phrases so they show the movement of thermal energy in order.

1. cup
   pot
   soup
   burner
   mouth

burner, pot, soup, cup, mouth

2. hot charcoal
   hamburger
   lit match
   grill

lit match, hot charcoal, grill, hamburger

3. warmed hands
   rubbing together
   bare hands

bare hands, rubbing together, warmed hands

4. hot air
   wet clothes
   dry clothes

wet clothes, hot air, dry clothes

5. mittens
   warm hands inside mittens
   cold hands wearing mittens
   campfire

cold hands wearing mittens, campfire, mittens, warm hands inside mittens

Harcourt

What Is Heat?

Lesson Concept

Energy is the ability to cause matter to change. Thermal energy is the energy of the movement of the particles inside matter. Thermal energy that moves from one thing to another is called heat.

Vocabulary

thermal energy (F39)   **heat** (F40)   **friction** (F41)

As you read the summary, fill in each blank with one of the vocabulary terms from above.

_____Friction_____ is the force between two moving objects that keeps the objects from moving freely. There are different kinds of energy.

All kinds of energy cause change. _____Thermal energy_____ is the kind of energy that moves particles in matter, and it is felt as

_____heat_____. Heat is the movement of thermal energy from one place to another. There are a number of ways to produce thermal energy. Rubbing things together, burning things, and mixing chemicals are three ways to produce thermal energy. Thermal energy is used in everyday life for things such as cooking and keeping people warm.

Underline the correct answer.

1. What are the particles in solids, liquids, and gases doing all the time?

A dissolving   **B** reacting   **C** increasing   **D** moving

Answer each question with one or more complete sentences.

2. Describe what happens to thermal energy when you touch a hot cup of cocoa. ___The thermal energy moves from the cup to your hand.___

3. Describe what happens to thermal energy when you touch a cold glass of juice. ___The thermal energy moves from your hand to the glass.___

Harcourt

Name _____

Date _____

What Gets Hot

Materials

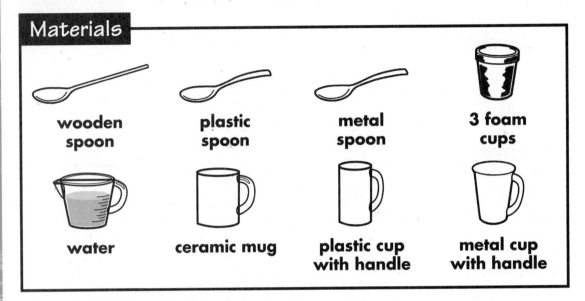

wooden spoon

plastic spoon

metal spoon

3 foam cups

water

ceramic mug

plastic cup with handle

metal cup with handle

CAUTION ## Activity Procedure

1 Use the chart below to **record** your **observations**.

2 Touch the three spoons. Are they hot or cold? **Record** what you **observe**.

3 **CAUTION** **Be careful with hot water. It can burn you.** Fill three foam cups with hot tap water. Set them on the table in front of you. Put one spoon in each cup. Wait one minute.

4 Gently touch each spoon. Which one is hottest? **Record** how hot each spoon is. Use words like *cool, warm,* or *hot.*

5 Next, fill each cup with hot tap water. Wait one minute. Then gently touch the handle of each cup. Which one is hottest?

6 Use the words you wrote in Step 4 to **record** how hot each cup handle is.

Spoons			Cups		
Wooden	Plastic	Metal	Ceramic	Plastic	Metal

Harcourt

Name _____

Investigate Log

Draw Conclusions

1. Study your Spoons chart. Did all the spoons get hot? Which spoon got the hottest? No. The wooden spoon didn't get hot. The metal spoon got the hottest.

_____

_____

2. Look at both charts. Which material got hot in both experiments? How did the plastic items change in the hot water? The metal got hot in both experiments. Both times the plastic got warm, but not as hot as the metal. (Plastic cups vary. This answer will depend in part on the kind of plastic used for the cup.)

_____

3. **Scientists at Work** As they test their ideas, scientists may change their **experiments** in small ways. Suppose you want to see if wood always stays cool when it is placed near heat. What kinds of wooden objects could you use in your experiment? Answers will vary, but could include wooden bowls and wooden rolling pins.

_____

Harcourt

Process Skills Practice

Experiment

You do an experiment to find out new information. An experiment is a kind of test.

Think About Experimenting

During a camping trip, the boys and girls did two experiments. First, they used a long, wooden stick to stir the potatoes that were roasting in the fire. Then, they used a long metal spoon. They found that the wooden stick stayed cool. The long, metal spoon heated up. For their second experiment, they took the cooked potatoes out of the fire. They wrapped one in foil and one in a piece of wool. They felt each of the potatoes several different times. They were surprised to learn that the wool kept the potato warm for a longer time than the foil did.

1. What information do you think the boys and girls were trying to gather when they did the experiment with the wooden stick and the metal spoon? They wanted to know if the two materials would heat up.

_____

2. What did they learn from the experiment? The metal spoon got hot, and the wooden stick stayed cool.

3. What information do you think they were trying to gather when they did the experiment with the potatoes? They wanted to know whether the foil or the wool would keep a potato hot for a longer time.

4. What did they learn from that experiment? The wool kept a potato warm longer than the foil did.

5. Why do you think the boys and girls were surprised at the information they gathered? Answers will vary, but may indicate that they expected the foil to keep the heat in, or that the wool would let the heat escape.

Harcourt

Summarize and Paraphrase a Selection

Thermal Heat Moving Through Things

A conductor allows thermal energy to move easily from one thing to another. Many things are made from materials that are good conductors. Cooking pots and pans are usually made of metal because metal allows thermal energy to move quickly to the food that is being heated. People often use wooden spoons to stir hot liquids on the stove because a metal spoon would heat up quickly and be too hot to handle. Materials that contain electrical parts are another example of good conductors. They keep the flow of thermal energy moving quickly.

An insulator, on the other hand, does not let thermal energy move easily through it. People use materials to insulate their homes. In the winter, insulation keeps heat from easily leaving the home. In the summer, insulation also helps keep warm air from entering the house. Mittens are good insulators because they keep body heat from easily leaving the inside of the mitten.

Write an outline for the above paragraphs.

I. Conductors allow thermal energy to move easily from one thing to another.

    A. Cooking pots are good conductors.

    B. Electrical parts use materials that are good conductors.

II. Insulators help keep thermal energy from easily leaving a material.

    A. Wall insulation keeps a home warm in winter.

    B. Wall insulation keeps a home from becoming warm in the summer.

    C. Mittens are good insulators.

Harcourt

How Does Thermal Energy Move?

Lesson Concept

Thermal energy can move when objects touch and particles bump into each other. It can move from one place to another in moving liquids or gases. Thermal energy from the sun moves by radiation.

Vocabulary		
	conduction (F46)	**conductor** (F47)
insulator (F47)	**convection** (F48)	**radiation** (F48)

As you read the summary, fill in each blank with one of the vocabulary terms from above. Then answer the questions that follow.

A _____conductor_____ lets thermal energy travel easily. An

_____insulator_____ is a material in which thermal energy doesn't move easily. The particles in heated liquids and gases can move from one place to another. Thermal energy that moves without touching anything, like thermal energy from the sun, moves by radiation.

1. Jessica is making scrambled eggs in a frying pan for breakfast. Do the

    eggs cook by convection or conduction? _____conduction_____

2. _____Convection_____ is the type of movement resulting from the way thermal energy moves in liquids and gases.

3. Thermal energy that moves without touching anything is called

    _____radiation_____ .

Name _____

Date _____

Measuring Temperature

Materials

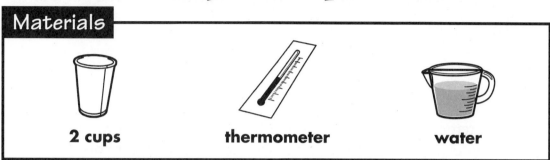

2 cups   **thermometer**   **water**

CAUTION Activity Procedure

1 Use the chart below.

2 **CAUTION** Be careful with hot water. It can burn you. Fill one of the cups with cold tap water. Fill the other with hot tap water.

3 Put the thermometer into the cup of cold water. **Observe** what happens to the liquid in the thermometer. On your chart, **record** the temperature.

4 Put the thermometer into the cup of hot water. **Observe** what happens to the liquid in the thermometer. On your chart, **record** the temperature.

5 Put the thermometer back into the cup of cold water. **Observe** what happens to the liquid in the thermometer. On your chart, **record** the temperature.

6 Wait one minute. Put the thermometer back into the cup of hot water. **Observe** what happens to the liquid in the thermometer. On your chart, **record** the temperature.

Water	Temperature
Cold water, Step 3	
Hot water, Step 4	
Cold water, Step 5	
Hot water, Step 6	

Harcourt

Name _____

Draw Conclusions

1. What happened to the liquid inside the thermometer each time you put the thermometer in the hot water? What happened when you put it in the cold water? _When the thermometer was put into the hot water the liquid moved up. When the thermometer was put into the cold water, the liquid went down._

2. Was the temperature of the hot water the same both times you **measured** it? What do you think caused you to get the measurements you got? _No. The hot water gave some of its thermal energy to the cooler air between the measurements._

3. **Scientists at Work** Scientists **measure** carefully. Write directions for how to measure temperature by using a thermometer. _Students' directions should include giving the thermometer time to reach the water's temperature and a description of how to read the thermometer._

Harcourt

Name _____

Date _____

Measure

Measuring is a way to observe things accurately. You can record the measurements you observe.

Think About Measuring

Christina bought a Christmas Cactus [*Schlumbergera*]. She learned that if she wanted the plant to bloom at Christmas, she would need to keep the plant where night temperatures would be between 10°C and 12°C (50° F and 55° F), beginning in November. Christina decided to measure the temperature in several areas in the house for three nights. Christina observed and recorded the temperatures at 8:00 P.M. each night. Her mother observed and recorded the temperatures at 11:00 P.M. After looking at the recorded temperatures, Christina chose the basement as the place to keep her plant.

		Basement Temp.	Kitchen Temp.	Living Room Temp.
Monday	8:00 P.M.	53°	68°	70°
	11:00 P.M.	51°	63°	68°
Tuesday	8:00 P.M.	55°	70°	70°
	11:00 P.M.	52°	65°	67°
Wednesday	8:00 P.M.	54°	67°	69°
	11:00 P.M.	50°	62°	66°

1. Why is it better to measure the temperature than to guess?

   Measuring is a way to prove the answers to questions; measuring is
   more accurate than guessing; measuring is a way for people who
   want to check the answers to take the same measurements.

2. Which of the areas where they were measuring temperature was the warmest at night in Christina's house? How do you know?

   The living room; the recorded temperatures were the highest there.

Harcourt

Use with page F51.

Name _____

Date _____

Identify Cause and Effect

Underline the causes and circle the effects in
the sentences below.

1. In thermometers the temperature of the air outside a glass
tube causes the liquid inside the tube to move up or down.
c: the temp....glass tube; e: liquid.....down

2. Inside a thermometer the liquid expands when it is warm and travels
up the tube.
c: when it is warm; e: liquid expands and travels up

3. When the liquid cools, the particles get closer together and sink down
the tube.
c: liquid cools; e: particles get closer together and sink down

4. When water reaches 0°C (32°F), it freezes.
c: water reaches 0°C (32°F); e: it freezes

5. When water reaches 100°C (212°F), it boils.
c: water reaches 100°C (212°F); e: it boils

6. Lead melts when its temperature reaches 327°C (620°F).
c: temp reaches 327°C (620°F); e: lead melts

7. When it gets cold in the winter, animals' fur becomes thicker.
c: cold in winter; e: animals' fur becomes thicker

8. Dressing lightly in hot weather helps people stay cool.
c: dressing lightly; e: helps people stay cool

9. Adjusting a thermostat helps control the temperature inside a building.
c: adjusting thermostat; e: helps control....building

10. A person with a fever has an increase in body temperature.
c: fever; e: increase in body temperature

Use with page F53.

Harcourt

How Is Temperature Measured?

Lesson Concept

Temperature can be measured with a thermometer. People control heat by wearing clothing and by using thermostats.

Vocabulary

thermometer (F52)

Underline the correct answer.

1. A thermometer is a tool used to measure ____.

   A how hot or cold something is   **B** how big something is   **C** how fast something is

2. In a liquid thermometer, ____ makes the liquid inside expand and move up the tube.

   A thermal energy   **B** cold air   **C** controlling heat

3. The liquid in a thermometer moves up the tube when it gets hot because ____.

   A it needs less space   **B** its particles don't move as fast   **C** it needs more space

4. When the liquid in a thermometer sinks down in the tube, it means that _____.

   A the particles are not moving as fast   **B** the temperature is rising   **C** the liquid is getting warmer

5. A dial thermometer uses a ____ instead of a liquid.

   A scale   **B** metal coil   **C** tube

6. One way to control heat inside a building is by using a ____.

   A thermometer   **B** Fahrenheit scale   **C** thermostat

Harcourt

Recognize Vocabulary

Underline the correct meaning for each word.

1. friction

   A conduction

   B convection

   C radiation

2. thermal energy

   A the energy of particles moving in matter

   B the way things move

   C the act of ice melting

3. heat

   A the energy of movement of matter

   B a particle that begins to burn

   C the movement of thermal energy from one place to another

4. conductor

   A a material in which thermal energy doesn't move easily

   B a material in which thermal energy moves easily

   C a way to keep particles from moving

5. insulator

   A something that moves thermal energy from one object to another

   B a material in which thermal energy can't move easily

   C a material that conducts radiation

6. thermometer

   A a tool used to measure how hot or cold something is

   B a tool used to measure whether or not a material is a good conductor

   C a tool used to measure particles in matter

Harcourt

Name _____

Date _____

Write a Business Letter

Persuasive Writing–Request

Use reference sources to find the address of a nursery, recycling center, or county agricultural board near you. Write a letter requesting information on setting up and maintaining a home compost heap. Use the letter format below to help you plan your writing. Share what you learn with your class.

Heading:

Inside Address:

Greeting:

Body of letter:

Hint: Remember to thank the person you are writing to for his or her time and assistance.

Closing:

Signature:

Harcourt

Chapter 3 • Graphic Organizer for Chapter Concepts

Forces and Motion

LESSON 1
MOTION

What Causes Motion?
a force, or a push or pull

What Is Motion?
a change in position from
one place to another

How Forces and Motion Interact

1. a force must be applied in
order to get
motion

2. not all forces cause
motion

How fast something moves is its
speed

The force that pulls us to Earth is
gravity

LESSON 2
WORK

What Is Work?
a force making something

move

These Things Are Work

1. riding a bike

2. lifting a box

3. planting a flower

These Things Are NOT Work

1. holding your books

2. pushing on a wall

3. reading a book

LESSON 3
SIMPLE MACHINES

What Are Simple Machines?
tools that help people do

work

The Six Simple Machines

1. lever

2. pulley

3. wheel and axle

4. inclined plane

5. wedge

6. screw

Harcourt

Measuring Pushes and Pulls

Materials

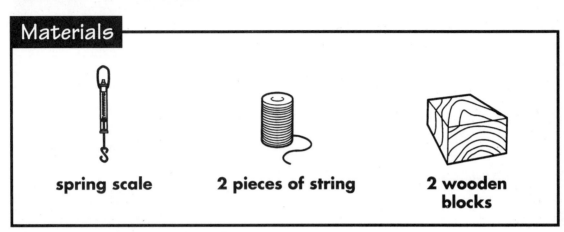

spring scale   **2 pieces of string**   **2 wooden blocks**

Activity Procedure

1 Work with a partner. One of you should hold one end of the spring scale while the other gently pulls on the hook. Read the number on the scale. The number is in newtons. Newtons measure pushes and pulls. **Record** the number.

2 Tie one piece of string around one of the wooden blocks. Tie the other end of the string to the hook on the scale.

3 Begin to pull on the spring scale. Pull as hard as you can without making the block move. **Record** the number on the scale.

4 Now pull hard enough to make the block move. **Record** the number on the scale. Carefully pull the block across the room. Watch the scale. Make sure the number doesn't change as you pull.

5 Repeat Step 4. This time, pull so that the number on the scale changes. **Record** your observations.

6 Tie the second wooden block to the first one. Repeat Steps 3 through 5. **Record** your observations.

Harcourt

Name _____

Draw Conclusions

1. How many newtons did it take to pull on the block without moving it? How many newtons did you use to move the block in Step 4?

Answers will vary depending on the block. It took more force to move the block across the floor than it did to pull on it without moving it.

2. How did you pull differently in Steps 4 and 5? In Step 4, the pull was steady. In Step 5, the pull was uneven. To make the numbers move up, the block had to be pulled faster or around in circles. To make the numbers go down, the block had to be pulled more slowly.

3. How did your results change when you added the second block?

It took more force, or newtons, to move both blocks.

4. **Scientists at Work** Scientists make charts to help them **interpret data**. Make a chart to organize the data you collected in this investigation.

Accept all reasonable charts.

Harcourt

Name _____

Date _____

Gather and Interpret Data

You can gather and interpret data for experiments. You can record your data.

Think About Gathering and Interpreting Data

Mark put a small stone in a cloth bag. Then he tied the bag to a spring scale and let it hang down. The scale measured 2 newtons pulling the stone down. In a second test, Mark added another stone to the bag. He estimated that the scale would now measure 3 newtons pulling the stone down. But the measurement was 4 newtons. As a third test, Mark took out both stones and put a smaller one in the bag. This time the scale measured only 1 newton.

1. Arranging data in a table can make it easier to interpret. Fill out the following table.

	First Test	**Second Test**	**Third Test**
Number or size of stones	one stone	2 stones	small stone
Newtons	2	3	1

2. How many newtons pulled the stone down the first time? __2 newtons__

3. In which test did the scale measure the most newtons? __the second test__

4. Mark estimated the number of newtons for his second test. Then he measured. Why was it a good idea for him to measure? __The measurement was more accurate than his estimate.__

5. What do you think Mark learned from his experiments? __Answers will vary, but should indicate an understanding that heavier weights are pulled down with more force.__

Harcourt

Identify Cause and Effect

The Games

The students in Mrs. Smith's class joined other students for an outdoor activity day at school. In the peanut race, Amanda had to push a peanut across the floor using her nose! The peanut moved very slowly. In the wheelbarrow race, John held Luis by his legs and pushed him forward toward the finish line. John accidentally pushed too hard, and Luis fell over. They both laughed. In another game, a group of students gathered in a circle and shot marbles. Samantha used her large marble to hit a smaller one, and the small marble shot across the circle. Samantha won for shooting her marble the farthest. The final game of the day was a large game of bumper ball. All the students sat in a circle. Each time that the cage ball came to a student, that student used his or her feet to bump the ball across the circle. It was a fun day.

What are some causes and effects in this selection? Finish the chart below.

Cause	Effect
Amanda pushed a peanut using her nose.	The peanut moved across the floor very slowly.
John pushed Luis in the wheelbarrow race.	Luis was pushed toward the finish line.
John accidentally pushed Luis too hard.	Luis fell over.
Samantha hit a small marble with a large marble.	The marble shot across the circle.
Samantha's marble moved the farthest.	Samantha won the game.
The cage ball moved toward a person.	That person bumped the cage ball across the circle.

Harcourt

Concept Review

How Do Forces Cause Motion?

Lesson Concept

Every motion is started and stopped by a force.

Vocabulary		
force (F66)	**motion** (F67)	**speed** (F69)
gravity (F70)	**weight** (F70)	

Underline the correct answer.

1. You see a flock of birds flying across the sky. You know that the motion of the birds was begun by ____.

   A a force   **B** gravity   **C** a change in position   **D** speed

2. Gravity is a ____.

   A lifting force   **B** squeezing force   **C** pushing force   **D** pulling force

3. The measurement of the pull of Earth's gravity on an object is ____.

   A length   **B** mass   **C** weight   **D** force

4. If you are comparing how fast two objects are moving over a certain distance, you are comparing their ____.

   A gravity   **B** force   **C** speed   **D** mass

5. To stop something from moving, you have to apply ____.

   A balance   **B** force   **C** speed   **D** weight

6. A change in position is called ____.

   A speed   **B** weight   **C** motion   **D** mass

Harcourt

Name _____

Date _____

Measuring Work

Materials

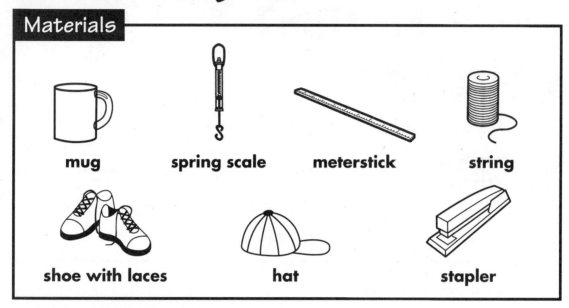

mug   spring scale   meterstick   string

shoe with laces   hat   stapler

Activity Procedure

1 Use the table on the next page.

2 Hook the mug onto the spring scale. Work with a partner. One of you should hold the meterstick on the table, with the 1-cm mark toward the bottom. The other person should rest the mug on the table next to the meterstick.

3 Gently lift the scale, and pull the mug off the table. Keep the scale and the mug next to the meterstick. **Record** the height you lifted the mug.

4 Read the number of newtons on the spring scale. **Record** the number.

5 Multiply the number of newtons you used times the distance you moved the mug. This is the amount of work that was done. **Record** this number in your table under the heading *Work*.

6 Repeat Steps 2 through 5, using each of the other objects. You may need to use the string to attach the objects to the spring scale. Lift each object the same distance you lifted the mug.

Harcourt

Distance × Force = Work			
Object	Distance (centimeters)	Force (newtons)	Work (newton-centimeters)

Draw Conclusions

1. Which object took the most force to lift? Which object took the least force to lift? Answers will vary depending on the objects used.

2. Describe the math you did in the table. You multiplied the force (measured by the scale) times the distance on the meterstick to find the amount of work performed. Note: Answers will be in newton-centimeters, since students measured the distances in centimeters.

3. In this investigation one of the measurements was kept the same. Which one was it? distance

4. **Scientists at Work** Scientists **infer** from data. Look at the data you collected. Infer how work is related to force. If the distance moved is the same, then the more force is used, the more work is done.

Harcourt

Name _____

Date _____

Infer

You can make an inference from data you collect when you do an experiment.

Think About Inferring

Using a spring scale and a string as shown below, Greg pulled a book across the top of a desk. It took a pulling force of 1 newton to move the book. Greg noticed there was a sheet of notebook paper under the book. He removed the sheet of notebook paper and tried again. This time it took 2 newtons to pull the book. Greg put the book on a sheet of construction paper. This time it took 3 newtons. Greg made the following table.

Force Needed to Move the Book	Surface
2 newtons	desk
1 newton	notebook paper
3 newtons	construction paper

1. What was different about the surfaces beneath the book? _____
There is a difference in _____

"slipperiness." _____

2. Which surface made the book easier to move? Why do you think this is so?
The notebook paper. It is the _____
most slippery. _____

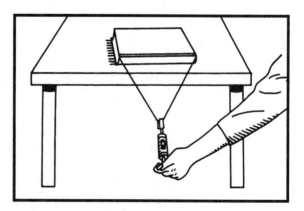

3. What can you infer from this experiment about the work you need

to do to move something over a surface? Explain. It takes less work _____

to move something over a slippery surface, because you don't _____

need to use as much force. _____

Harcourt

Name _____

Date _____

Arrange Events in Sequence

Rewrite the sentences so that they are in order. Look for clue words such as *first, then, next, after,* and *last* to help you.

Next, Dale began to push large amounts of snow with the shovel.

First, Dale put on his hat and gloves.

Finally, after one hour, Dale had cleared all the snow from the driveway.

Then, Dale chose a shovel from the garage.

First, Dale put on his hat and gloves.
_____

Then, Dale chose a shovel from the garage.
_____

Next, Dale began to push large amounts of snow with the shovel.
_____

Finally, after one hour, Dale had cleared all the snow from the driveway.
_____

_____

Write a paragraph that describes how a man moved a wagonload of dirt from his front yard to his garden. Use clue words such as *first, then, next, after,* and *last.*

_____

_____

_____

_____

_____

_____

Harcourt

What Is Work?

Lesson Concept

In science, work is done when a force moves an object.

Vocabulary

work (F74)

Answer each question with one or more complete sentences.

1. Jack worked very hard trying to push the piano in his living room. But the piano didn't move. Would a scientist say that Jack had done some

work? Explain why or why not. No, if an object doesn't move, no

work is done.

2. Jack's older sister helped him. They moved the piano to the other side of the living room. Would a scientist say that Jack and his sister had done

some work? Explain why or why not. Yes, a scientist would say that

Jack and his sister had done work, because the force they used

moved the piano.

3. Emily used 60 newtons to lift her baby sister 1 meter in the air.

How could you figure out the amount of work done? Multiply the force

used by the distance the object moves.

4. How much work did Emily do? 60 newton-meters

Harcourt

Name _____

Date _____

Moving Up

Materials

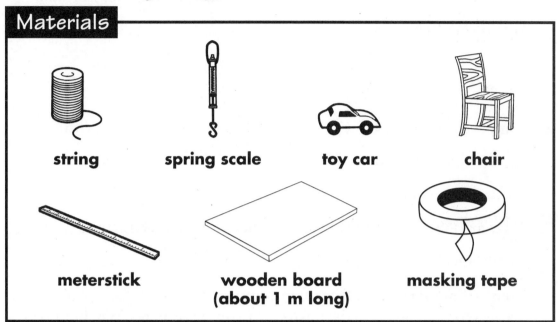

string   spring scale   toy car   chair

meterstick   wooden board (about 1 m long)   masking tape

Activity Procedure

1. Using the string, attach the spring scale to the toy car. With the spring scale, slowly lift until the bottom of the car is at the same level as the seat of the chair. Read the spring scale, and **record** the number.

2. Use the meterstick to **measure** how high you lifted the car. **Record** this number, too.

3. Prop up one end of the board on the seat of the chair. Tape the board to the floor so the board does not move.

4. Now place the toy car at the bottom of the board. Slowly pull the car to the top of the board at a steady rate. As you pull, read the force on the spring scale. **Record** it.

5. **Measure** the distance you pulled the car up the board. **Record** it.

Harcourt

Name _____

Draw Conclusions

1. Multiply the force you **measured** by the distance you moved the toy car. How much work did you do without the board? How much work did you do with the board? Answers will vary depending on the materials used, but the same amount of work should have been done both with and without the board.

2. **Compare** the force used without the board to the force used with the board. Which method used less force? With the board less force was used.

3. **Compare** the distance the car moved each time. Which method used less distance? The car moved less distance without the board.

4. **Scientists at Work** Scientists often **compare** their data. Compare your answers to Question 1 to the answers of your classmates. What did you find out? The answers are the same, which means the same amount of work was done. The answers may not be identical due to experimental error, but they should be close.

Investigate Further Repeat the activity using boards of several different lengths. **Record** the results. Did you use less force with longer boards or shorter ones?

Harcourt

Name _____

Date _____

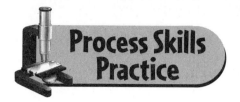

Compare

When you compare, you look at two or more events to see how they are alike and how they are different.

Think About Comparing

Andre was visiting his Uncle Arthur in West Virginia. Behind his uncle's house was the steepest hill Andre had ever seen. He decided to climb it. He started at the bottom and began climbing straight up. Halfway up the hill, Andre was tired and couldn't go any farther. He heard Uncle Arthur laughing. "Follow the cowpath," shouted Uncle Arthur. Andre saw that the cows had worn a zig-zag path up the hillside. He took the cowpath the rest of the way. It was a longer distance than climbing straight up. But it turned out to be much easier.

1. Compare Andre's climb straight up the hill to the experiment you did in the investigation. Climbing straight up is like pulling the toy car attached to the spring scale. Andre is moving less distance, but using more force.

2. How is the cowpath like something you did in the investigation? The cowpath is like the board in the investigation.

3. Compare the two methods of climbing. Which method uses less force? The cowpath method uses less force.

4. Which method of climbing the hill uses the most distance? The cowpath method uses more distance.

5. Which method of climbing the hill uses more work? Both methods use the same amount of work.

Harcourt

Name _____

Date _____

Use Context to Determine/Confirm Word Meaning

Each of the underlined words has more than one meaning. Write the definition for each word, based on how it is used in the sentence.

1. Bobby set a school <u>record</u> for highest score in a basketball game.
   record: a top performance _____

   Janet had to <u>record</u> her day's activity in her diary.
   record: to write down _____

2. You can use a <u>spring</u> scale to measure force.
   spring: elastic device _____

   Many new plants grow in the <u>spring</u>.
   spring: season following winter _____

3. A doorstop is a kind of <u>wedge</u> that has two inclined planes stuck back-to-back.
   wedge: piece of metal, wood, etc., with a thick back and a thin edge _____

   Marie politely asked for another of <u>wedge</u> cake.
   wedge: V-shaped piece _____

4. Joseph used a <u>screw</u> to hold together his wagon.
   screw: a simple machine _____

   After Jim was finished with the jar, his mother asked him to <u>screw</u> the lid back on.
   screw: to turn or twist _____

Harcourt

Use with page F79.

Concept Review

What are Simple Machines?

Lesson Concept

Simple machines do not change the amount of work, but they reduce the amount of force needed to do the work, or they change the direction of the force.

Vocabulary

simple machine (F78)   **lever** (F78)   **inclined plane** (F79)

Underline the correct answer.

1. A ____ is an example of an inclined plane.

   A pulley   **B** rod   **C** lever   **D** board

2. When you pull something up an inclined plane you use less ____ than you use to pick it straight up.

   A energy   **B** force   **C** distance   **D** strength

3. Suppose you use a pulley attached to a pole to pull up a flag. What does the pulley do to the direction of the force?

   A changes   **B** keeps the direction   **C** makes no change
       the direction   the same   in the direction

4. Which of the following activities is NOT being done with a simple machine?

   A turning a doorknob **B** prying open   **C** cutting out a picture
       to open a door   a paint can   from a magazine

5. A pair of scissors is a compound machine, because ____.

   A it is made of several **B** it has a lever   **C** one blade is a wedge
       simple machines

Harcourt

Recognize Vocabulary

In the space provided, write the term in Column B that best fits the definition in Column A. Use each term only once.

Column A

1. _____ force

   a push or a pull

2. _____ motion

   a change in position

3. _____ speed

   the measure of how fast something
   moves over a certain distance

4. _____ gravity

   the force that pulls objects toward
   each other

5. _____ weight

   a measure of the pull of gravity
   on an object

6. _____ work

   the measure of force it takes to
   move an object a certain distance

7. _____ simple machine

   a tool that makes work easier

8. _____ inclined plane

   a flat surface set at an angle to
   another surface

9. _____ lever

   a bar that moves on or around
   a fixed point

Column B

A motion

B work

C simple machine

D force

E gravity

F inclined plane

G lever

H speed

I weight

Harcourt

Name _____

Date _____

Write a Poem About a Machine

Expressive Writing–Poem

Write a poem about riding a bicycle or a theme park ride. In your poem, tell about the simple machines that make up the bicycle or the theme park ride. Include sensory words to describe the feeling of riding. Use the word web below to help you plan your poem.

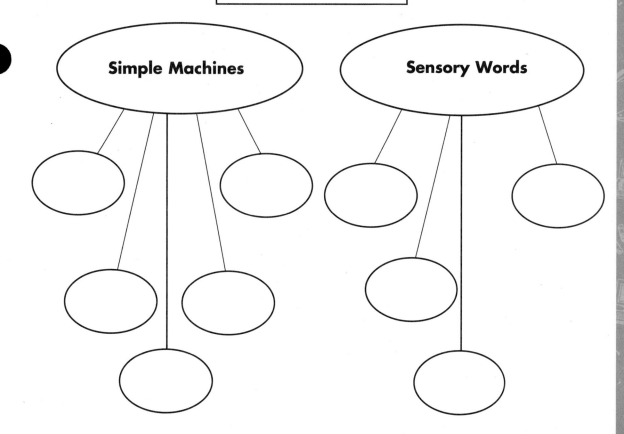

Harcourt

Unit Experiments
Grade 3

Harcourt

Name _____

Date _____

Experiment Log

Use these pages to plan and conduct a science experiment to answer a question you may have.

1 Observe and Ask Questions

Make a list of questions you have about a topic. Then circle a question you want to investigate.

_____

_____

2 Form a Hypothesis

Write a hypothesis. A hypothesis is a suggested answer to the question you are investigating. You must be able to test the hypothesis.

_____

_____

3 Plan an Experiment

Identify and Control Variables

To plan your experiment, you must first identify the important variables. Complete the statements below.

The variable I will change is _____

_____

The variable I will observe or measure is _____

_____

The variables I will keep the same, or control, are _____

_____

_____

Harcourt

Name _____

| Develop a Procedure and Gather Materials | Write the steps you will follow to set up an experiment and collect data.

_____

_____

_____

_____

_____

_____

_____

_____

_____

_____

| Materials List | Look carefully at all the steps of your procedure and list all the materials you will use. Be sure your teacher approves your plan and your materials list before you begin.

_____

_____

_____

_____

_____

_____

_____

_____

_____

Harcourt

Name _____

4 Conduct the Experiment

Gather and Record Data Follow your plan and collect data. Make a table or chart to record your data. Observe carefully. Record your observations and be sure to note anything unusual or unexpected. Use the space below and additional paper, if necessary.

Interpret Data Make a graph of the data you have collected. Plot the data on a sheet of graph paper or use a software program.

5 Draw Conclusions and Communicate Results

Compare the hypothesis with the data and the graph. Then answer these questions.

Do the results of the experiment make you think that the hypothesis is true?

Explain. _____

_____

How would you revise the hypothesis? Explain. _____

_____

_____

What else did you observe during the experiment? _____

_____

_____

Prepare a presentation for your classmates to communicate what you have learned. Display your data table and graph.

Harcourt

Plant Growth and Water Sources

1 Observe and Ask Questions

Do different liquids affect how a plant grows? For example, will plants watered with tap water grow taller than plants watered with tap water mixed with vegetable oil, tap water mixed with dishwashing detergent, or tap water mixed with vinegar? Make a list of questions you have about plant growth and different liquids. Then circle the question you want to investigate.

Will plants watered with tap water grow taller than plants watered with
_____

vegetable oil and water, dishwashing detergent and water, or vinegar and
_____

water?
_____

2 Form a Hypothesis

Write a hypothesis. A hypothesis is a suggested answer to the question you are investigating. You must be able to test the hypothesis.

Plants watered with tap water will grow taller than plants watered with
_____

vegetable oil and water, dishwashing detergent and water, or vinegar and
_____

water.
_____

3 Plan an Experiment

To plan your experiment, you must first identify the important variables. Complete the statements below.

Identify and Control Variables

The variable I will change is the type of liquid I give the plants.
_____

The variable I will observe or measure is how much the plants grow.
_____

Harcourt

Name _____

Experiment Log

The variables I will keep the same, or *control*, are the type of plant, amount
of liquid, amount of sunlight, type of soil, and temperature.

_____

Develop a Procedure and Gather Materials

Write the steps you will follow to set up an experiment and collect data.

a. Use a pencil to make two small holes in the bottoms of four foam cups.

b. Label the cups as follows: Tap Water, Water and Detergent, Water and
Vinegar, Water and Vegetable Oil.

c. Put potting soil into each cup until it is about two-thirds full. Use the
balance to be sure that the same amount of soil is in each cup.

d. Place the plants in the potting soil, and add a small amount of the type
of water shown on the cup label. Be sure to add the same amount of
water to each cup.

e. Place the cups on a tray or in a pan. Then place the pan or tray in a
sunny place.

f. Each day, add a small amount of the type of water shown on the cup label.
Be sure to add the same amount of water to each cup.

g. Observe the plants each day for two weeks. Use a centimeter ruler to
measure and record the heights of the plants.

Use extra sheets of blank paper if you need to write down more steps.

Materials List Look carefully at all the steps of your procedure, and list
all the materials you will use. Be sure that your teacher approves your plan
and your materials list before you begin. foam cups, balance, measuring
cup, 4 plants, tap water, dishwashing detergent, vinegar, vegetable oil, potting
soil, marker, centimeter ruler, tray or pan

Harcourt

Name _____

4 Conduct the Experiment

Gather and Record Data Follow your plan and collect data. Use the chart below or a chart you design to record your data. **Observe** carefully. **Record** your observations, and be sure to note anything unusual or unexpected.

Plant Observations

	Height (mm)						
	Day 1	Day 2	Day 3	Day 4	Day 5	Day 6	Day 7
Tap Water							
Water/ Vegetable Oil							
Water/ Detergent							
Water/ Vinegar							

	Height (mm)						
	Day 8	Day 9	Day 10	Day 11	Day 12	Day 13	Day 14
Tap Water							
Water/ Vegetable Oil							
Water/ Detergent							
Water/ Vinegar							

Harcourt

Observe

Interpret Data

Make a graph of the data you have collected. Plot the data on a
sheet of graph paper or use a software program.

5   Draw Conclusions and Communicate Results

Compare the **hypothesis** with the data and graph, and then answer
these questions.

1. Based on the results of the experiment, do you think the hypothesis is
true? Explain. Students should justify their responses with data and
observations.

_____

_____

2. How would you revise the hypothesis? Explain. Students may revise their
hypotheses to match the results of the experiment more closely.

_____

_____

3. What else did you observe during the experiment? Encourage students to
use their notes and to be as specific as possible.

_____

_____

Prepare a presentation for your classmates to **communicate** what you have
learned. Display your data table and graph.

Investigate Further Write another hypothesis that you might investigate.

Plants grow better with pond water than with tap water.

_____

_____

_____

_____

Harcourt

Acid Rain and Plants

1 Observe and Ask Questions

How does acid rain affect plants? For example, does a plant that is exposed to acid rain change in any way? Make a list of questions you have about acid rain and plants. Then circle a question you want to investigate.

Does being exposed to acid rain cause changes in a plant?

What changes occur in a plant that takes in acid rain?

2 Form a Hypothesis

Write a hypothesis. A hypothesis is a suggested answer to the question you are investigating. You must be able to test the hypothesis.

Plants that are exposed to acid rain will not grow as well as plants that are

not exposed to acid rain.

3 Plan an Experiment

To plan your experiment, you must first identify the important variables. Complete the statements below.

Identify and Control Variables

The variable I will change is how often each plant is sprayed with vinegar,

which will be used to represent acid rain.

The variable I will observe or measure is the color and number of the

plant's leaves.

The variables I will keep the same, or *control*, are the type of plant, the

amount of sunlight, the type of soil, and the temperature.

Harcourt

Experiment Log

| Develop a Procedure and Gather Materials |

Write the steps you will follow to set up an experiment and collect data.

a. Place the plants in a sunny spot.

b. Label four plants as follows: Control, Daily, Every Other Day, Weekly.

c. On Days 1, 3, 5, 7, 9, and 13, give the Control plant one full spray of

tap water.

d. Pour vinegar in a spray bottle. CAUTION: Be careful when working with

vinegar. Wear safety goggles when working with acids.

e. On Days 1 through 14, give the plant marked Daily one full spray of vinegar.

f. On Days 1, 3, 5, 7, 9, 11, and 13, give the plant marked Every Other Day one

full spray of vinegar.

g. On Days 1 and 8, give the plant marked Weekly one full spray of vinegar.

h. Observe the plants daily. Record all observations.

_____

_____

_____

Use extra sheets of blank paper if you need to write down more steps.

| Materials List | Look carefully at all the steps of your procedure, and list
all the materials you will use. Be sure that your teacher approves your plan
and your materials list before you begin.

four identical plants, 2 spray bottles, vinegar, tap water, paper, pencil

_____

_____

_____

_____

Harcourt

Name _____

4 Conduct the Experiment

| Gather and Record Data | Follow your plan and collect data. Use the chart below or a chart you design to record your data. **Observe** carefully. **Record** your observations, and be sure to note anything unusual or unexpected.

Observation Log

Plant Label	How the Plant Looks						
	Day 1	Day 2	Day 3	Day 4	Day 5	Day 6	Day 7
Daily							
Every Other Day							
Weekly							
Control							

Plant Label	How the Plant Looks						
	Day 8	Day 9	Day 10	Day 11	Day 12	Day 13	Day 14
Daily							
Every Other Day							
Weekly							
Control							

_____

_____

_____

Harcourt

Experiment Log

Observe

| Interpret Data | Make a two-column chart. Label the columns *Plant* and *Change*. List the plant labels in the first column. Compare your observations from Day 1 and Day 14. Summarize your findings in the second column.

5 Draw Conclusions and Communicate Results

Compare the **hypothesis** with the data and chart, and then answer these questions.

1. Based on the results of the experiment, do you think the hypothesis is true? Explain. Students should justify their responses with data.

_____

_____

2. How would you revise the hypothesis? Explain. Student may revise their hypotheses to more closely match the results of the experiment.

_____

_____

3. What else did you **observe** during the experiment? Encourage students to use their notes and to be as specific as possible.

_____

_____

Prepare a presentation for your classmates to **communicate** what you have learned. Display your data table and chart.

| Investigate Further | Write another hypothesis that you might investigate.

Accept testable hypotheses.

_____

_____

_____

Harcourt

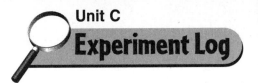
Decomposition of Trash in Landfills

1 Observe and Ask Questions

Substances that we do not or cannot recycle often end up in landfills. Landfills are places in which trash is buried. Some trash in landfills decays, or decomposes. Some trash does not decompose. Make a list of questions you have about trash that is buried in landfills. Then circle a question you want to investigate.

What types of trash decompose when buried in landfills? What types of

trash don't decompose in landfills? How deep is trash buried in a landfill? Does

the depth of burial affect whether trash will decompose?

_____

2 Form a Hypothesis

Write a hypothesis. A hypothesis is a suggested answer to the question you are investigating. You must be able to test the hypothesis.

Plastic will decompose more slowly than paper and organic matter will.

_____

3 Plan an Experiment

To plan your experiment, you must first identify the important variables. Complete the statements below.

| Identify and Control Variables |

The variable I will change is *the type of trash.*
_____

The variable I will observe or measure is *the decomposition of each type*
_____

of trash.
_____

Harcourt

Experiment Log

The variables I will keep the same, or *control*, are the size of each piece of
trash, the depth at which each piece is buried, the burial location, and the
time each piece remains buried.

| Develop a Procedure and Gather Materials |

Write the steps you will follow to set up an experiment and collect data.

1. Collect different types of trash—paper, plastic, aluminum, and organic
   matter.

2. Find a place on the school grounds to bury the trash where it won't be
   disturbed.

3. Make sure each piece of trash is the same size. Put each piece into a
   separate plastic mesh bag and securely close each bag.

4. Dig a hole for each type of trash. Make sure the holes are the same size.

5. Put one type of trash into each hole, and cover each hole completely
   with soil.

6. Use labeled craft sticks to mark the type of trash buried in each hole.

7. Dig up the trash once a week and observe the trash to see if it has
   changed. Record your observations.

8. Rebury the trash.

9. Repeat steps 7 and 8 for at least a month.

Use extra sheets of blank paper if you need to write down more steps.

Harcourt

Materials List Look carefully at all the steps of your procedure, and list all the materials you will use. Be sure that your teacher approves your plan and your materials list before you begin. safety goggles, gardening gloves, trowel, trash, craft sticks, permanent marker, plastic mesh bags like those that hold onions or fruits

4   Conduct the Experiment

Gather and Record Data Follow your plan and make careful observations. **Record** your **observations,** and be sure to note anything unusual or unexpected.

Observation of Decomposition

Type of Trash	Week 1	Week 2	Week 3	Week 4

Harcourt

Name _____

5 Draw Conclusions and Communicate Results

Compare the **hypothesis** with your observations, and then answer these questions.

1. Based on the results of the experiment, do you think the hypothesis is true? Explain. Students should justify their responses with their observations and results.

2. How would you revise the hypothesis? Explain. Students may revise their hypotheses to match the results of the experiment more closely.

3. What else did you **observe** during the experiment? Encourage students to use their notes and to be as specific as possible. Observations might include that trash does not change much when it is buried.

Investigate Further Write another hypothesis that you might investigate.
The depth of burial will change the rate of decomposition. The temperature of the soil will change the rate of decomposition. The length of time trash is buried changes the rate of decomposition.

Harcourt

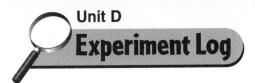
Air Pressure and Temperature

1 Observe and Ask Questions

Because air has weight, it presses on things. This is called air pressure. Sometimes air presses harder against things than it does at other times. Changes in air pressure are related to changes in air temperature. Make a list of questions you have about the relationship between air pressure and air temperature. Then circle a question you want to investigate.

How is air pressure related to air temperature?

Does colder air press against things with more force than warmer air does?

Does an increase in air temperature result in a decrease in air pressure?

_____

_____

_____

_____

2 Form a Hypothesis

Write a hypothesis. A hypothesis is a suggested answer to the question you are investigating. You must be able to test the hypothesis.

Cold air pushes harder against things than does warm air.

_____

_____

3 Plan an Experiment

To plan your experiment, you must first identify the important variables. Complete the statements on page WB322.

Harcourt

Identify and Control Variables

The variable I will change is _the temperature inside the containers._ _____

The variable I will observe or measure is _how air pressure changes with_ _____

temperature. _____

The variables I will keep the same, or *control*, are the _size and shape of_ _____

each container and the amount of water in each container. _____

Develop a Procedure and Gather Materials

Write the steps you will follow to set up an experiment and collect data.

a. _Measure 1 cup of cold tap water._ _____

b. _Pour the water into a clean, 1-liter clear plastic bottle. Put the top on._ _____

c. _Measure 1 cup of hot tap water._ _____

d. _Pour the water into a second clean, 1-liter clear plastic bottle._ _____

Put the top on. _____

e. _Observe what happens to each bottle._ _____

CAUTION: Be careful when filling the bottle with hot tap water.

Use extra sheets of blank paper if you need to write down more steps.

Materials List Look carefully at all the steps of your procedure, and list all the materials you will use. Be sure that your teacher approves your plan and your materials list before you begin. _safety goggles; cold tap water;_ _____

hot tap water; measuring cup; 2 clean, empty, 1-liter clear plastic bottles with _____

screw tops _____

_____

_____

Harcourt

4 Conduct the Experiment

| Gather and Record Data | Follow your plan. Make and **record** careful **observations. Draw** a picture of each can after the experiment is completed.

Bottle with Cold Tap Water

Bottle with Hot Tap Water

Observations _____

_____

_____

_____

_____

Harcourt

Experiment Log

5 Draw Conclusions and Communicate Results

Compare the **hypothesis** with your observations, and then answer these questions.

1. Given the results of the experiment, do you think the hypothesis is true? Explain. _Students should justify their responses_ _____

with data and observations.

_____

_____

_____

2. How would you revise the hypothesis? Explain. _Students may_ _____

revise their hypotheses to match the results of the experiment

more closely.

_____

_____

_____

3. What else did you **observe** during the experiment? _Encourage students_ ____

to use their notes and be as specific as possible.

_____

_____

Prepare a presentation that includes your drawings of the two bottles. **Communicate** what you have learned in this experiment.

| Investigate Further | Explain how you might use your results to make an instrument to measure changes in air pressure.

Accept reasonable ideas.

_____

_____

_____

_____

_____

_____

Harcourt

The Freezing Point of Water

1   Observe and Ask Questions

What substances change the freezing point of water? Will mixing substances such as salt, sugar, or baking soda in ice water raise or lower its temperature? Make a list of questions you have about water's freezing point and how different substances affect it. Then circle a question you want to investigate.

Does mixing salt, sugar, baking soda, baking powder, or artificial

sweetener with freezing water change its temperature? Do salt,

sugar, baking soda, baking powder, or artificial sweetener raise or

lower the temperature of ice water? Does water's freezing point change

if these or other substances are dissolved in the water?

2   Form a Hypothesis

Write a hypothesis. A hypothesis is a suggested answer to the question you are investigating. You must be able to test the hypothesis.

All the following substances added to water will change its freezing

point: salt, sugar, baking soda, baking powder, and artificial sweetener.

3   Plan an Experiment

To plan your experiment, you must first identify the important variables. Complete the statements below.

Identify and Control Variables

The one variable I will change is the type of substance I dissolve in the

ice water.

The variable I will observe or measure is how the temperature of the

water changes.

Harcourt

Name _____

Experiment Log

The variables I will keep the same, or *control*, are ___size of container,___

___amount of water and ice, amount of solid to dissolve, type of water,___

___thermometer, clean spoons.___

Develop a Procedure and Gather Materials

Write the steps you will follow to set up an experiment and collect data.

1. Label a container as follows: Ice Water Only

2. Fill the container with crushed ice to (2 cm) from the top. Measure water into the container to the same level. CAUTION: Wipe up any spills immediately.

3. Stir the water to make it as cold as possible.

4. Hold the end of a thermometer below the surface of the water for one minute.

5. Read and record the temperature to the nearest °C .

6. Label a container "Ice Water + Sugar" and repeat steps 2 and 3.

7. Carefully measure 3 tablespoons of sugar into the container and stir the mixture to dissolve as much of the sugar as possible. CAUTION: Wipe up spills immediately.

8. Repeat steps 4 and 5.

9. Repeat steps 6–8 four more times, labeling a container and dissolving each of the following substances: Baking Soda, Baking Powder, Salt, and Artificial Sweetener.

Use extra sheets of blank paper if you need to write down more steps.

Harcourt

Name _____

Experiment Log

Materials List Look carefully at all the steps of your procedure and list all the materials you will use. Be sure that your teacher approves your plan and your materials list before you begin.

6 containers, measuring cup, crushed ice, water, marker, ruler, stirring

spoon, clock, tablespoon, sugar, baking soda, baking powder, salt,

artificial sweetener, thermometer

4 Conduct the Experiment

Gather and Record Data Follow your plan and collect data. Use the chart below or a chart you design to record your data. **Observe** carefully. **Record** your observations and be sure to note anything unusual or unexpected.

Observations: Freezing Point of Water with Added Substances

Substance	Temperature after 1 min in °C
(Tap) Water and Ice Only	
Ice Water + Sugar	
Ice Water + Baking Soda	
Ice Water + Baking Powder	
Ice Water + Salt	
Ice Water + Artificial Sweetener	

Harcourt

Name _____

Experiment Log

Interpret Data

Make a graph of the data you have collected. Plot the graph on a sheet of graph paper or use a computer graphing program.

5 Draw Conclusions and Communicate Results

Compare your **hypothesis** with the data and graph, then answer these questions.

1. Based on the results of the experiment, do you think the hypothesis is true? Why or why not? Students should justify their responses with data and observations.

2. How would you revise the hypothesis? Be specific.
Students may revise their hypotheses to match the results of the experiment.

3. What else did you **observe** during the experiment?
Encourage students to use their data and to be as specific as possible.

Prepare a presentation for your classmates in order to **communicate** what you have learned. Display your data table and graph.

Investigate Further Write another hypothesis about water and how it freezes that you might investigate.

What substances change the boiling point of water?

_____

_____

_____

_____

_____

_____

Harcourt

Solar Heat

1 Observe and Ask Questions

What does color have to do with the temperature of objects that are placed in sunlight? For example, which colors absorb the most heat from the sun? Make a list of questions you have about solar energy. Then circle a question you want to investigate.

Will light-colored objects placed in sunlight absorb more heat than

dark-colored objects will?

Which color will absorb the most solar energy—blue, yellow, white, or black?

Which colors will reflect the most heat?

2 Form a Hypothesis

Write a hypothesis. A hypothesis is a suggested answer to the question you are investigating. You must be able to test the hypothesis.

Light-colored objects will absorb more heat than dark-colored

objects will.

3 Plan an Experiment

To plan your experiment, you must first identify the important variables. Complete the statements below.

Identify and Control Variables

The variable I will change is the color of the containers that I place in

sunlight.

The variable I will observe or measure is the temperature of the water

inside the containers.

The variables I will keep the same, or *control*, are the size and type of

container, the amount of water, the time period for measuring

temperatures, the amount of sunlight.

Harcourt

Experiment Log

Develop a Procedure and Gather Materials

Write the steps you will follow to set up an experiment and collect data.

a. Cover the surface of the test area with newspaper to collect spills.

b. Paint each can, both inside and outside, a different color. Use yellow, white, blue, and black paint. The inside and outside of each can should match.

c. After the cans dry, measure the same amount of water into each can until it is nearly full of water.

d. Tear off a piece of plastic wrap large enough to cover the top of each can, and fasten it around the can with a rubber band.

e. Place the four cans in a place where they will get as much sunlight as possible.

f. Measure and record the room temperature or surrounding air temperature.

g. Every 30 minutes, remove the plastic wrap from each can and measure and record the temperature in each can as well as the room or surrounding air temperature.

NOTE: The thermometer should be at room temperature before each measurement.

h. Measure and record the temperature of each can at 30-minute intervals for 3 hours.

Use extra sheets of blank paper if you need to write down more steps.

Materials List Look carefully at all the steps of your procedure, and list all the materials you will use. Be sure that your teacher approves your plan and your materials list before you begin.

4 metal cans, all the same size (soup or vegetable cans), 4 colors of flat paint (including yellow, white, blue, and black), newspapers, paintbrushes, plastic wrap, rubber bands, water, measuring cup, thermometer(s), clock or watch

Harcourt

Name _____

4 Conduct the Experiment

| Gather and Record Data | Follow your plan and collect data. Use the table below or a table you design to record your data. **Observe** carefully. **Record** your observations, and be sure to note anything unusual or unexpected.

Color and Temperature Observations

Can Color	Temperature (taken every 30 minutes)					
	Measurement Times					
	30 min	1 hour	1 hour 30 min	2 hours	2 hours 30 min	3 hours
no can—air temperature only						
Yellow						
White						
Blue						
Black						

Other Observations

_____

_____

_____

_____

_____

_____

_____

Harcourt

Interpret Data

Make a graph of the data you have collected. Plot the graph on a sheet of graph paper, or use a software program.

5 Draw Conclusions and Communicate Results

Compare the **hypothesis** with the data and graph, and then answer these questions.

1. Based on the results of the experiment, do you think the hypothesis is true? Why or why not? Explain. _Students should justify their responses with data and observations._ $8 \times 6 = 6 + 6 = 100$

2. How would you revise the hypothesis? Explain. _Students may revise their hypotheses to match the results of the experiment more closely._

3. What else did you **observe** during the experiment? _Encourage students to use their notes and to be as specific as possible._

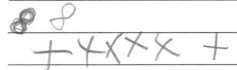

Prepare a presentation for your classmates to **communicate** what you have learned. Display your data table and graph.

Investigate Further Write another hypothesis about solar heat that you might investigate.

Accept testable hypotheses.

Harcourt